PRAISE

"With lyrical and evocative prose, Joseph Hurka not only captures here his mentor, my late father, the short story master Andre Dubus, he also renders with grace and tenderness the often unconscious need and yearning a young person has for an authentic teacher... a beautiful and deeply moving memoir."
ANDRE DUBUS III

"This is a book that honors the memory of one of America's greatest storytellers while reminding us that writers are characters themselves, unlikely heroes, flawed companions, both born of and broken by the world."
JENNIFER MILITELLO, POET LAUREATE OF NEW HAMPSHIRE

"Tobias Wolff has described the work of the late writer Andre Dubus as 'an unapologetically sacramental vision of life in which ordinary things participate in the miraculous, the miraculous in ordinary things.' The gift of this vision returns to us in *On the Invisible Palm of God*, a remarkably wise, intimate, and luminous memoir by Joseph Hurka, Dubus's one-time student and longtime friend."
SUSAN DODD, AUTHOR OF *MAMAW*

"This eloquent memoir of apprenticeship, friendship, and tribute to fiction writer Andre Dubus (pere) reminds me of Gorki's classic account of Tolstoy or more recently Tom Grimes's of Frank Conroy. Torches of craft and spirit are shared, and then passed on."
DEWITT HENRY, AUTHOR OF
DO I DREAM OR WAKE? (LONG POEMS)

ABOUT THE AUTHOR

Joseph Hurka is the author of the memoir, *Fields Of Light: A Son Remembers His Heroic Father*, a winner of the Pushcart Editors' Book Award. His short fiction and memoir writing have been featured in numerous literary journals, and in the collection, *Graceful Lies*. He has also written for *Journeys Home*, a National Geographic Books travel publication. He teaches at Tufts University and lives in southern New Hampshire.

ABOUT THE AUTHOR

ON THE INVISIBLE PALM OF GOD

JOSEPH HURKA

www.vineleavespress.com

On the Invisible Palm of God
Copyright © 2025 Joseph Hurka

All rights reserved.
Print Edition
ISBN: 978-3-98832-153-4
Published by Vine Leaves Press 2025

No parts of this publication may be reproduced, stored in a retrieval system, or transmitted in any form or by any means, electronic, mechanical, photocopying, recording, or otherwise, without the prior written permission of the copyright owner.

This book is sold subject to the condition that it shall not, by way of trade or otherwise, be lent, resold, hired out, or otherwise circulated without the publisher's prior consent in any form of binding or cover other than that in which it is published and without a similar condition including this condition being imposed on the subsequent purchaser. Under no circumstances may any part of this book be photocopied for resale.

Grateful acknowledgment is given to the following:
The Literary Estate of Andre Dubus, for permission to quote from his many written works and from his interview with WHYY's public radio host Terry Gross, on Fresh Air, 1991.
WHYY and NPR, for permission to quote from Andre Dubus, Fresh Air With Terry Gross interview, 1991.
The literary estate of James Alan McPherson for permission to quote from his essay, "Forward to the Collected Stories of Breece Pancake," in *A Region Not Home: Reflections from Exile.*
Michael Blumenthal, for permission to quote from his poem "The Dangers of Metaphor" in *Against Romance*, Viking/Penguin, 1987.
An excerpt from *On the Invisible Palm of God* appeared in the online literary journal, *The Woven Tale Press*, in 2024.

Cover design by Jessica Bell
Interior design by Amie McCracken

So we fix our eyes not on what is seen, but on what is unseen, since what is seen is temporary, but what is unseen is eternal.

2\. Corinthians 4:18

For Andre

AUTHOR'S NOTE

To protect the privacy of those involved in this story, I have occasionally changed names, appearances, and addresses; I've changed some business names, as well.

PART ONE

CHAPTER ONE

It is a sultry summer evening, so warm that there, with the screens open to Haverhill, Massachusetts, many human voices seem close, surrounding me. The home I am standing in is on a steep hill on Broadway, perhaps half a mile from the Merrimack River and looking out over the rural street and fields and forest. I imagine men fishing; I hear women laughing, cooking somewhere close. There are the sounds of adults conversing, relaxing, on a deck on the hill, and of boys on skateboards thundering and scraping on a tar driveway. A hawk drifts over some trees, just beyond the road below, where the valley opens; beneath his steady wings there is a tangled, shallow cleft of summer green, and telephone lines soaring. Into this evening Andre Dubus rolls, in his wheelchair, into his living room.

There is a ramp built over two stairs and he glides down on that plywood; he catches the banister post easily with his right hand and turns onto the beaten, hardwood floor. The room has windows the full length of the wall, and Andre talks about the beautiful sky, the hawk, the Red Sox. His voice is at medium range, fast and excited, his hair and beard salt-and-pepper gray, whitening now. Time and pain, the shock of amputation, have done this. It is 1998, and in a month he will be sixty-two.

We banter, a profane, happy recital of jokes. Sometimes, for emphasis, he'll exaggerate his native Louisiana drawl. He backs his wheelchair up close to the hunter-green couch with its heavy cushions, and makes sure that the cushions are ready and firm for his back, clapping them like old war buddies. He removes the brace of the chair for his right, atrophied leg, sidles the chair up close to the couch, then anchors it and transfers his body, settling himself in an upright position against the cushions. He leans forward and puts his right leg up on a stack of pillows that he has prepared; he is wearing red sweatpants that are folded at the stump of his left leg and tied off with a bandana. All his motions are done smoothly, with the practice of the nearly twelve years of his crippling.

A large mug of Diet Coke sits beside him on a small white side table—I've brought the drink from the kitchen for him, along with the Saltine crackers he must have during Red Sox games. Andre has just showered; he smells of Old Spice anti-perspirant: citrus, cedarwood. He wears a worn, light-blue t-shirt across his broad chest. The ice of the Diet Coke rattles as he drinks. He is *squared away,* as he puts it, in Marine terms; he chides me, merriment in his eyes, about the ease of my mobility, calls me a *fucking biped.* I sit on the couch opposite him; the television is across from us on a raised platform. His red-socked remaining foot sticks out at me in its plastic brace from over the pillows, and the stump strains upward a moment as he adjusts his position, and I think of the car coming toward him, headlights bright and growing over a late-night highway, and the terror of it moves through me but I keep up the humor, tell him at least I'm not a *Goddamn invalid,* a pain in the ass to everybody, and he calls me a bastard, happily, removing the "r" like a true New Englander—*bastid.*

He hits the remote and the Red Sox are already into their first at bat, Nomar Garciaparra coming up. *C'mon Nomar, c'mon man,* Andre says. The great shortstop goes through a ritual adjustment of his batting gloves—a process that takes many moments—then steps into the box and steadies into his stance. The Red Sox are playing the Athletics: the sounds of the crowd are first-inning-scattered, expectant; the voice of the sportscaster assured. There is a sense of beginning here, that something might start with the Red Sox at any moment, some spark of new life. And my old teacher, my mentor and friend, Andre Dubus, somehow *is* America, on this waning summer evening with his happiness and his resilience and the sounds of humanity all around him.

We watch Garciaparra poised and determined at the plate, thirty-five miles away, the pitcher beginning his wind-up, the Fenway crowd hushed, waiting.

•

Sixteen years before this I was twenty-one, a guitar player at night in bars, an occasional journalist, a college dropout. I worked days on the eastern side of Haverhill with my father, a consulting engineer and Czech native; I had been Dad's right-hand man since I was fourteen at his business, Hurka National Laboratories. Dad developed products for the sports and hardware and communication industries, and we had an additional business making fiberglass kayaks and rowing shells. During this January of 1982, we were located in an old airplane hangar at a small airport next to the Merrimack, right on the Groveland line. It was a bright, cold morning, and through the hangar window I saw snow blowing across the runway, and there were planes, a gleaming Cessna 172

Skyhawk and a Piper Cherokee, tethered to the ground right outside our back door.

We wore white paper coats to keep our clothes clean of the various chemicals we used to develop Dad's products. We were creating a batch of prototype ski tips for a prominent ski company—this was a new, popular item then: small, hook-like extensions that ski racers fixed to the tips of their skis to help deflect oncoming gates in slalom courses. Our original take on the product was the material Dad employed for it—urethane, an elastic substance that seemed to grow back magically when you dented it; the material had never been used in this application before. Skiing was in our blood: Dad once raced on the international circuit for the Czech National Team, and he'd brought me up skiing; I had eventually raced for a Division I team at the college that I had attended, briefly, in New Hampshire. The urethane tips promised some much-needed income for us: if the company liked the new product, we would set up for a large production.

•

The hanger was expensive to heat, so we'd built a small, plastic tent within the space, a rig of two-by-fours and plastic sheeting—an interior room. Everything felt thrown together, temporary, as neat as we tried to keep it. We'd recently made a fast and difficult move from nearby Newburyport. A crooked landlord, wanting to sell off the old mill building we were in, had suddenly shut off the electricity for all his tenants. The tenants were collectively suing the man, but that didn't help Hurka National Laboratories with our immediate need. Dad had discovered this airplane hangar, and we had moved our essential equipment into it and put the rest of our materials into storage. The move, done with the help of a few friends who occasionally worked with us, had been exhausting. It had drained us financially as well; it was something of a breaking point, something we were struggling back from.

Before me, in the hanger, was a group of small, rectangular epoxy molds, silver in color. I took one, opened it, made sure it was clean and waxed thoroughly. Then snapped it together again, injected liquid urethane into it, thick and red, until it slightly overflowed. My father beside me did the same with another mold. We put them on a turntable Dad had developed for this process, and ran them under a set of heating lamps. You injected more of the molds and put them on the Lazy-Susan and by the time the first ones got around to you again, they had cured. You opened the first mold and now there was a solid ski tip inside, and you pulled it out and trimmed the excess urethane with a razor, and put the finished piece into a metal bin that was already full—a pile of red sharks' teeth fished from the chemical sea—and went back to cleaning and waxing and injecting the molds.

•

We worked two more hours and finished a set of the prototypes at noon, then cleaned up and went into the city for lunch. When we returned, we stood for a few minutes in our small office. Dad brought out a brochure he'd picked up at a local institution called Bradford College. I knew of the college, of course—I had passed by it hundreds of times on my way back and forth to the rural town of Boxford where we lived. I had never really given much thought to the place, honestly: my mother had told me that I'd once attended a kindergarten there staffed by college students. On the front of the brochure was a glossy picture of a stately old brick building with six white columns, ivy running up the walls.

I knew Dad wanted me to return to school, to finish the college education I'd started. He never pushed you into things: he presented you with information to help you make a decision and left you to it. But ours was a family that revered education: my father had an advanced degree in Ballistics and Military Sciences from the Military Academy of Hranice, Czechoslovakia; my mother had graduated from Northwestern with degrees in French and Spanish. I wasn't sure, now, what I wanted to do. I'd attended New England College, just west of Concord, New Hampshire, and I'd enjoyed the ski racing and college girls and the journalism and literature classes I was taking, but because I'd worked with Dad throughout my years as a teenager I was also conscious of how tough his business had been of late—financial security was sometimes fleeting for an inventor and consultant—and how much my education was costing. I was on numerous scholarships and grants, but when I thought about it, I couldn't justify the money spent on my education when I was still without true direction. After my knee blew out in a race during my sophomore year and my ski career—small as it was—was finished, I felt completely without a rudder. I thought maybe I'd make a living from freelance writing, somehow, or perhaps would be some sort of investigative reporter. What I dreamed most about was music: I loved writing songs on my guitar and performing them anywhere someone would listen—I'd played in many taverns and small coffeehouse gatherings in New Hampshire, and these days when I wasn't performing for income I was working, nights, on an album in a couple of small, nearby recording studios.

I carried with me a memory of my father dropping me off at NEC one fall day, and how I felt for him as he drove away—he was fifty-five then and had suffered from stress and heart complications; he'd had a heart attack a few years before. Dad had many, significant inventions to his name: the first all-fiberglass ski, the first molded edges and foam cores in skis; he'd developed plastic snow mats for ski areas and urethane foam technology for the inside of ski boots and winches made of Kevlar for the European communications industry. Like many inventors, even when his initial ideas held a patent, Dad had lost many of his creations to big-money corporations that simply changed minor aspects of his inventions and "created" their own products. Dad was trying to run Hurka National Laboratories and hoping that one of his ideas would take off so that he could help give a decent future to me and my brother, Chris, ten years my junior. I wanted to get back to Massachusetts to help him, and more selfishly I couldn't see where college was taking me and wanted a break from it. When I decided to leave my studies, I wasn't sure I would ever return. I think Dad sensed this truth in me, and that he was angry at himself for our financial situation and saddened by my decision.

So now I watched my father as he put forward this college option. He would help me with tuition money. I could go part-time, see if I liked it.

"Joseph," he said, his Czech accent still heavy (when he used my full name this way it always meant something of import was coming), "you've been a big help to me. But building and shipping boats and dealing with investors and business isn't the future you want. You like art and writing and music, and you could pay attention to those things if you studied at

Bradford. Nothing would change except that with the studies you would have a plan 'B' going—some future income from a degree—just in case you need it."

There was a release in this, this truth-telling, a sense that we both recognized that my future would be elsewhere. He'd found a few interesting classes, he told me; a printed list was folded inside the brochure. He pointed them out to me: there was one for creative writing, another in early American literature—these looked like things I might enjoy, he said. He left it all with me to look over while he went to turn on the heating lamps and check and clean the molds and fire up the next round of prototypes. I read over the glossy brochure and the listings and sensed, for the first time since I'd left school, that something waited for me here, that this was a right move, a solid direction. I stared out the small window we had in the office. I could see, from there, the parking lot with its snow drifts, and the black Merrimack, flowing slowly down toward the steel Groveland bridge. The sky was winter stark, an infinite, bright blue.

CHAPTER TWO

On the other side of the old mill city, in the area that was once a town called Bradford—now absorbed into the larger metropolis of Haverhill—there was the college, a campus of eighteen acres frosted with snow, the dignified brick buildings at the entrance with their large white columns. If you'd just arrived from the fast traffic of Route 125 and the dust and cement winter cold of the city below, you felt you were suddenly in another, quieter century. You stepped inside Academy Hall to a kind of friendly old calm; there was a front parlor which used, long ago, to be a waiting room for men who came to court when the college was still a women's finishing school. The room was now like a museum, with photographs behind glass of those young women—at dances, in their dorm rooms with their triangular Bradford flags on the wall, and building snowmen with delight on the lawn outside; they were all just spirits now, with this room holding some of the few physical reminders of their time on earth.

You walked by the waiting room and at the reception office to your right a secretary told you where registration was. The halls were busy with people, and you felt the curvature of the wooden floor beneath your legs, the ceilings high above you. There were old chandeliers up there and the pleasant sound, everywhere, of the place in use, the floorboards straining and creaking. In the registration office, you were given a sign-up sheet and directions: past the dining room then, old and varnished wood and formal, always busy with one function or another. Here were young women bundled for the cold, laughing together about something said in a first class. They were attractive, with brief, flirtatious eyes—they glanced down at the guitar case you held (you couldn't leave your precious Guild F-50 in the cold)—it was good to be around college girls again—and you followed them out a back door. The winter early-afternoon sky was pink and orange, many students gathered here in the modest student center, a small wooden building with walls of windows and a grill and pool tables. Here was the campus, stretched out beneath a recent snow, unsullied by the pollution of the nearby highways and the business of the city: trees cradled the white, and there were many student cars in the parking lot, dusted with snow and ice.

The Dorothy Bell building was my destination—a flat, modern structure with a veined marble facade and floor-to-ceiling windows. I was going to try and join—I looked down at the registration form I'd been given—*English 318: Fiction Writing Seminar.* I stepped inside (through an art gallery—I liked the fact that you had to go through an art gallery to get to your classes) and in the library itself, the bright afternoon sounds of winter had transformed into the respectful hush of so many students at the start of a new semester—hunched over long, varnished tables, walking through the stacks of books. I went up the spiral staircase to the second floor, where the fiction class was about to meet in a room called Seminar D.

•

Andre Dubus came into his classroom—bearded, scarf, frayed jean jacket, a blue chamois shirt, jeans, cowboy boots. He had a Louisiana drawl—he was a laughing, jousting *presence*. He wore a brown Akubra hat that he plucked off his head and dropped on the front table; four long tables were pushed together in the class to make a square. Beyond them and the students already seated, you could see what was called Tupelo Pond, a small, black, iced-over body of water just below the floor-to-ceiling glass. I stood to the side; I'd met an old high school friend just outside the room—she'd told me happily that *she* was in this class, and that I *must* take it, too—and now she lobbied on my behalf for Andre to let me join. He liked her and laughed good-naturedly at her efforts and said he had room. I stumbled then through what I hoped was a respectful explanation: I really wanted to be in the course, I told him, but I had a musical audition in Boston in an hour and a half—would it be all right for me to miss this one day?

There was a certain, quick reticence in Andre's eyes: who was this character who had asked to be in his class, and now was leaving? It is amazing, looking back on it, that he still let me in. But he nodded and signed my form and said, "Okay, man, see you next time," and turned to his class of students, and I had a sharp, sudden sense of regret—I had immediately liked him and the atmosphere of the room and wanted to remain; the feeling stayed with me as I went down the stairs and out to my car.

•

The audition was in a broken-down recording studio near Boston University. I'd seen an ad in *The Boston Globe* for singer-songwriters: a group of producers were looking for talent. I thought this might be a route to help get my album made. But the place looked dark and sleazy: the recording board was dated, and heavy curtains were everywhere to baffle sound and perhaps to make the heating more efficient; there were no windows to be seen. Two men interviewed me, all of us sitting beneath a set of theatrical stage lights; I played them some of my songs, and they said they thought I could be the next Billy Joel—all I had to do was pony up three thousand dollars, and they would take care of the rest of the expenses for my first record.

I walked out to Beacon Street with my guitar after, night coming, dirty snow by the sidewalks. I found my old Chevy Chevette waiting for me, honest and alone, under a streetlamp. I got onto Storrow Drive, angry at the waste of time and the crookedness I seemed to see everywhere now, in this business with these "producers" or with the Newburyport landlord who had given Dad and me and the other tenants such trouble. Always, there seemed to be someone reaching into your pockets, taking your energy or time, indifferent to your condition, trying to pull some profit, some blood, out of you—feeding off you. Unbridled hope, rationalizations—these things could drift you toward bad shores, a lesson I seemed to be getting a heavy exposure to lately.

Traffic moved slowly through the darkness and funneled me onto the 93 deck over the city. The skyscrapers of Boston on this winter evening were bright, twinkling. And then the cars began to move more freely, and slowly I forgot the sleazy audition, and I was heading north, thinking of the class I'd been fortunate enough to join with the professor named Andre. I thought of the man's honest laugh and the intelligence and quickness of his eyes. And of Seminar D: how just before Andre Dubus had arrived, as students were finding their seats, I'd been struck, looking out the windows, by all the light, the feeling that you were suspended just a few feet above campus.

CHAPTER THREE

Andre Jules Dubus II was at this time hardly known outside of tight, respectful literary circles. He had authored a novel, *The Lieutenant,* and three collections of stories, *Separate Flights*, *Adultery and Other Choices*, and *Finding A Girl In America*. His short fiction, prior to being collected, had been published in *The New Yorker* and *Playboy,* and in numerous literary quarterlies, including *Ploughshares* and *Sewanee Review.* Still, the fame that had come to other writers with similar accolades eluded Andre, primarily because he was not one to play political games or "network"—a word he hated—or to acquiesce to an editor's poor judgment just for publication. He wasn't a darling of any particular literary set.

He was forty-five when I met him: he was making a thin salary and living in campus faculty housing with his wife, Peggy Rambach, also a writer and Bradford professor, and their infant daughter Cadence. He'd had two previous marriages and was the father of four more children. He taught five classes per semester—an overwhelming amount of work for someone who is engaged, also, in a serious life of art. Andre had been offered a great deal more money, he once told me, to teach at Princeton, where his teaching load would have undoubtedly been more respectful of his fiction—but he'd turned it down because Haverhill, this old northeastern mill city, was his home now, a place of friends and family that he loved, and it was also where much of his material was born. And Andre was a man who relied on a set routine to steady him, to give him a bedrock for his art and life.

He'd come from Cajun country, born to a Cajun-Irish family in Lake Charles, Louisiana, in 1936. He grew up in nearby Lafayette and attended a Christian Brothers school and then McNeese State College, where he'd graduated in 1958 as a journalism and English major. He married his first wife, Patricia Lowe, soon after, and went into the Marines, rising to the rank of captain. In the early sixties, with Pat and their children—Nicole, Andre III, Jeb, and Suzanne—he moved from California to Iowa City, IA, to attend the Iowa Writers' Workshop. He wrote in Hollywood for a time—developing, with Burt Lancaster, a screen adaptation of *The Lieutenant;* the film was never completed. The job at Bradford College came in 1966.

·

During these first winter afternoons in 1982 we read our stories aloud in Seminar D, and this new teacher of mine listened, sitting at the center of the front table, his head tilted back, his hands hanging by his sides, his eyes closed. Often, he got up and stepped quietly around the classroom; one of my first memories is of Andre standing, leaning against one of the cement window-columns, wearing the worn denim jacket, as a student read her story aloud. Andre patted his beard and looked at the light on the iced-over water. His eyes narrowed and he closed them and bowed his head with concentration. He took our work seriously, and because of his interest and concentration we took our writing seriously, also: you always felt, when you workshopped, that the professor's full attention was with you.

When he was jotting something on the board for us to remember, he held the stick of chalk carefully, as if a little unfamiliar with it, as if wielding some fine, foreign instrument. As you watched him you quickly understood that, for all his bawdy humor and frequent profanity, he was also deeply sensitive, thoughtful, empathetic. His eyes were green-wet, alive with emotion. A student asked, in one of our first classes together, why fiction stories often had such grim endings. Andre spoke of the false impulse, frequently demonstrated in American storytelling and particularly in American cinema, to come up with a "positive" ending rather than the ending the characters had earned; many times writers surrendered to the pull of entertainment, he said, instead of following the natural psychological and active progression of their characters. He took up the chalk and wrote on the board: *All art is affirmative, because it ensures that we can endure being mortal.* He looked at the quote a moment. "That's me," he said, quietly, a little distracted by his thoughts. "I said that."

He could be seriously reflective; he could sometimes explode with joy and laughter. He could be quickly, visibly angry—at concepts, politics, sophistry: his expressive eyes did nothing to hide the tumult of emotions within. In these first years that I knew him a restless undercurrent churned in him, a kind of separation from the present that he longed for, a need to get back to the internal world he was creating. He was a gifted and enthusiastic conversationalist. He was respectful of others by nature and often seemed in awe of those he met—of anyone, college janitor or college president: he engaged quickly with them, asked intelligent, probing questions about their lives, listened to their stories. You sensed that above all else he cared for the *humanity* of others, as he joked or considered or suggested, as he philosophized and offered moments of wisdom. He was deeply and earnestly Catholic. It wasn't unusual to hear him swear about the Vatican, about "all the poor people" who could be housed in that "fucking exalted space." I never saw him judge another human being by their economic station or their status. It didn't matter to Andre what station of life others occupied—a person's character was what he cared about.

Mid-winter was gray outside the classroom windows: snow came occasionally from clouds that stretched over the college. In our workshops we read our prose haltingly, nervously at first, then with growing confidence as we realized the professor had a true interest in what you were doing. We had to write at least five pages per week; class met twice weekly and we read on a revolving basis, in time slots we had signed up for. Most of us closed our eyes as we listened to the stories of our peers, following the lead of our teacher. Then usually we would talk about the stories passionately, the room becoming embroiled in debate. "Isn't this *great?*" Andre said, happily, during one such melee. "We're all having a fight about a bunch of characters who don't even exist."

CHAPTER FOUR

There was a painting near the door of Seminar D that our professor referred to often. The artist had created a bridge over water, a small house, a heavy blue sky and sun, wildflowers in the foreground.

"Take one element of the painting out," Andre told us, in one of our first classes, "or make that aspect smaller or larger, and the whole composition falls apart. In fiction, it is the same, everything based on *balance, proportion*." We were talking that day about a young woman's story and Andre asked her now for the manuscript. She handed it to him and he undid her paper-clip, and took the manuscript apart, page by page, laying it in a chronological line on the long front table, facing toward the class.

"You can learn a lot from looking at a story visually," he told us, "and thinking about how much attention you're giving to each section of the narrative." He went through the scenes, describing what was happening in each, his blue-jeaned, bearded form moving against the blackboard. His index finger pointed through the pages. "The trouble you're having here is that the climax of your story, which should take up the most energy, is written at about the same depth as the other scenes—all of your scenes occupy about a page and a half, and the climatic section only two. This ending section should have at least three or four pages devoted to it. You see?" His right hand made arcs in the air now as he described the course the story needed to take. "You just need to give that section more attention, more specificity, and the power of the story will change right in front of you."

The author and the rest of us nodded at this, looking at the pages—it was clear, the way our teacher explained it.

Always beside Andre, on that front table, there was a record book where he kept notes about us—he wrote in a steady, artistic cursive with looping capital letters—and a small volume of Chekhov's stories. Often, he picked up the Chekhov to read us a character description or an atmospheric passage to demonstrate how Chekhov brought characters to life, how he balanced and gave proportion to his work. He often quoted Chekhov's saying that a single moment can change a life forever. And he wrote another of Chekhov's admonitions on the board: *Don't tell me the moon is shining: show me the glint of light on broken glass.*

"Always remember the importance of light," Andre told us. "The contrast of light and dark in a scene can give insight into character and theme. Artists call this *chiaroscuro.*" It was a word we would hear many times in the coming semester.

·

After creative writing, we retired to the campus snack bar with Andre, just a few steps away from the library. We leaned into the counter with our orders, burgers and fries and Cokes, and sat at the round tables; usually it was crowded, with the radio playing current hits and the sounds of pool: the snapping of billiard balls, the dropping and throaty rolling sounds as they fell through the tables. I always tried to sit near Andre to make sure I heard what he was saying.

"Hemingway did the same thing you guys are doing when he was in Paris," he told a group of us, after the class where he'd focused on the idea of proportion. "He looked at paintings in museums and made connections between what the painters were doing—the balances they were striking—and what he was doing on the page. He was constantly training himself."

One coed—my former high school companion—said she'd read an article that criticized the workshopping process, which said classes such as ours created "cookie cutter" stories that just imitated one another. She wondered how our mentor felt about this.

"There are a lot of purists who put down the idea of classes and workshopping," Andre said. "Usually these are critics rather than artists. Somebody should ask them—what were Hemingway and Fitzgerald and Stein and all the rest doing on the Left Bank? They were authors, getting together, discussing stories. It was the same thing you're all doing. That's how you learn, man."

He had a way of making us feel that we were embarked on an important journey—I think he felt that we were. We talked in the Bradford snack bar until the light fell, until the orbs of the campus lights outside hovered beneath the violet winter sky like small spaceships.

[illegible] through the tables, I [illegible] to make sure I heard what he was saying.

[illegible] did the [illegible] you [illegible] he [illegible] up of us after th[illegible]

[illegible]

[illegible] connection [illegible]

[illegible]

CHAPTER FIVE

On the bottom floor of the library there was a reading room, and in it a table with a display of faculty books. One of these was Andre's *Separate Flights,* the cover art earth-tone browns and golds, with arrows on a diagonal plane going in different directions to indicate the spiritual flights of the characters within. I took the book from the display table, sat on the firm blue couch by the window, and began reading. The glass windows were floor-to-ceiling here, too; outside the winter-late afternoon was gray and cobalt-blue, and when I glanced up I could see the parking lot and the iron fencing at the edge of the campus and South Park Street beyond.

I fell into the first story, the novella *We Don't Live Here Anymore.* It was easy to imagine the setting—I was in Haverhill, in a fictionalized neighborhood nearby; the story is narrated by Jack Linhart, a college professor, and focuses on two couples: Jack and his wife, Terry, and their friends, Hank and Edith. Both couples have children, and both are broken by affairs; eventually, each man is having an affair with the other's wife. It is dense, unsparing stuff: you find yourself alternately appalled by the selfishness of the characters and the choices they make—particularly with regard to the neglect of their children—and impressed with the author's honesty, and with the realization that, given certain circumstances and rationalizations, you might be capable of similar, appalling choices.

I read a long time and was with the characters, *within* them, really—such was the effect the author's writing had on you. Finally, I looked at my watch and went and checked the book out from the friendly librarian named Betty: she was in her late forties, with big trusting eyes behind glasses. "Oh, his work is *wonderful*—and he's such a *good* guy," she told me, looking down fondly at the cover. I went out to the Chevette and put the book on the seat beside me, and sometimes I looked over at it as I drove south on Kingsbury Avenue; Kingsbury became Main Street in Boxford, and the houses were more sporadic as I went through the forested darkness, seeing the white of Chadwick Pond through trees and then the frosted slopes of Far Corner Golf Course. In front of the center store in West Boxford there was the wooden Indian, glazed white now in winter—I'd hung out many summers here with friends as a boy. But I wasn't thinking of my summers or the past. My head was still in Andre's story, with his characters, and I was imagining how it must be to write a story like that. Up onto Ipswich Road now and by the sprawling Witch Hollow farm, I turned down into Valley Road and drove past old middle-class homes until the lights of our garrison came through the trees. In the kitchen I greeted Dad and Mom and Chris; my brother was eleven then. I had a late dinner of meatloaf and potatoes that my mother heated up for me, and Chris told me about his day at school, and how afterward he'd been sledding with some of his buddies, the massive jumps they'd built. Mom asked me about the college and I told them all about Andre's class and the novella of Andre's I was reading, and my father listened quietly, happily, with his steady eyes.

I read until I slept that night: I dreamt of the characters, and in the early morning I took up the reading again and had to go back a few paragraphs because I realized in my dream I'd made up sentences and scenes that were not in the actual story.

Driving from the airplane hangar to classes at Bradford that day, still thinking of *We Don't Live Here Anymore,* I thought of how paltry my knowledge was of contemporary fiction. This was a new world for me: I would have to do some heavy reading in the Bradford library to have a little more depth of understanding. I would ask Andre for suggestions. I'd read writers of the near-past: Hemingway, Steinbeck, some of Faulkner—*As I Lay Dying* and *The Wild Palms* were favorites; I'd loved Mark Twain's *Huckleberry Finn* and Rudyard Kipling's stories since I was a boy. Though I'd been an athlete and a musician and never quite eclectic enough for the intellectual crowd in high school, I'd absorbed Shakespeare and Dickens and Hawthorne and Hardy in literature classes, and remembered how affected I'd been by *Black Boy,* Richard Wright's powerful memoir. I'd loved the grace and intelligence of Rachel Carson's writing—my parents kept all her books in their library—and I'd always loved poetry: I thumbed often through a slim, cracked, leather-bound volume my mother had owned since her childhood, with poems by Longfellow, Whitman, Edna Vincent Millay, James Joyce, and many others. There were drawings and photos of these writers at the start of each work. I'd stared at their faces, brought them to life in my imagination. I lived in the language they created; when I read the work of great artists the *music* of their writing haunted me for days.

I sensed in the work of my new teacher the same greatness I'd felt from the classic authors of fiction I'd read—a similar completeness of characters and depth; a similar humanity, and the ability to take a local world and make it universal. Recently, I'd finished re-reading the stories in Hemingway's *The Snows of Kilimanjaro,* a book I'd returned to again and again; the work of Andre Dubus, I realized now, was to me every bit as penetrating, as powerful, as the Hemingway.

•

Inspired, I set out to finish some stories of my own, often borrowing the form and pacing of my new mentor. I'd attempted stories before, and mostly they had turned out to be little more than a few ambitious passages strung together. Now, the immediacy of Andre's presence and lessons, and the example of his work, suddenly made me understand how I could approach subjects and characters I'd always wanted to write about, how I could bring the stories to some sort of conclusion. Fiction had to be born from some reality, Andre told us—from something that moved you, made you uncover a new truth about yourself or your surroundings—and it needed to center on some moral trial. In the early evenings after my classes, I sat at the long tables in the Bradford library, in that hushed dimness and with the white grounds outside: cars in the parking lot and sketches of trees and dormitories. There was a protected sense to this place, a quiet that invited thought and creativity. The lamps above me were circles of light and as the evening darkened, they reflected more precisely in the windows. And I was moving into my recent past, writing about a late night after a music gig in Rowley, an incident I'd experienced at a small diner off Route 133 in Ipswich; it was extraordinary, the way as I worked, I could remember the smell of rain on tar outside the diner, the bright light within that was in contrast to the late spring night.

In fiction I was liberated to simplify things, to make them work toward my ending. My main character, the central point of consciousness, transformed then from a musician to a simple diner employee, a high-school student, a guy sweeping the floor. I called him Ansel. As Ansel worked two prostitutes came through the door. My character watched the reactions around him—the disdain of other women, the quiet, lustful eyes of some truckers. Writing now, I could remember the silver interior of the place and the red-cushioned booths and the hissing sounds of cooking; I could remember the light dresses the prostitutes wore and the way they didn't seem to mind the attention they attracted, but bowed their heads and spoke quietly together. I could see the smiles and subtle vulgarity of a group of male teenagers over by a dark window—one making a circle with the fingers of one hand, poking the index finger of his other hand through—how their reflections were like sly ghosts in that glass.

My character held the door for the women as they left. It was a gesture of chivalry; also, a small part of Ansel hoped to make some connection with these good-looking women whose liberal sexuality was a mystery to him. One of them told him, "You're the first gentleman I've met tonight"—the same line I'd heard from one of the real prostitutes, as I'd held the diner door for them. Outside, beyond the cement steps, trucks rushed by on the wet pavement, indifferent to the small drama that had gone on in the bright, temporary world of the diner.

It was a simple story but because of Andre's teachings, my writing was more focused than it had ever been. I called it "The Diner," and thought there probably wasn't much to it, but I read it to the class on my appointed day, anyway, nervously. Andre was looking at me with quiet consideration when I finished. He asked the students to look at how I established the night through Ansel's point of view, as the boy looked out the window of the diner; he took my manuscript and read passages of my work aloud. My peers nodded and said they liked the story, too, pointing out parts they had enjoyed. I hadn't expected any praise, frankly—I didn't know what I'd expected, beyond just a general survival of the experience. At my previous college I'd taken a literature course with the writer Russell Banks, who'd once returned a blue book exam to me by saying, *Joe, you should think seriously about writing.* The memory came back to me now, as I saw Andre's eyes and the way the class reacted.

CHAPTER SIX

In those first weeks of the spring semester I worked at the hangar with Dad in the mornings—we were now putting together large orders of the ski tips—and then went to afternoon classes and afterward, if I wasn't playing a gig in Newburyport, or Rowley, or Haverhill, I sat at the long Bradford library tables, working on my fiction and my other homework. Being in that place during daylight, because of all the glass walls, was like being in some placid outpost: the sun came through the forest branches during the end of those January and February days and you saw the various hues of light across the ice of Tupelo Pond, orange to pink to blue, and the snow edging the rails of the bridge there. I read books for a class called *Concepts of American Literature;* the professor, Dr. Anne Sloane, had us reading Nathaniel Hawthorne's *The Scarlet Letter.* I'd read this book in high school, as well as Hawthorne's *The House of the Seven Gables;* I remembered a field trip a class of mine had taken to see the old house in Salem, how it stood stark and worn by tourism, gardens of chrysanthemums, impatiens, begonia, the harbor stretching behind.

Here in the Bradford library I looked through the library stacks for more Hawthorne and found a volume of his short stories. I opened the pages and came onto "Young Goodman Brown." I sat in an upper cubicle, reading. Here was the same New England forest that I'd grown up in and knew, the earthy smells and the wind of it, the density of the trees, though in Hawthorne's version there was an additional, strange light of human evil—a gathering of corrupted souls—showing through the branches. I was struck with how, consistently, Hawthorne identified American duplicity: a precarious human community and strict habits of propriety set against the deepest, natural primal yearnings.

Andre's class was changing the way I took in stories. I was no longer going along just for the ride: I noted Hawthorne's choices, the way he moved his scenes, the balance he gave to each. The dark decisions that Hawthorne's characters were left with seemed modern and immediate to me: in a slightly different context, they might have happened yesterday, in this America. I sensed in what I was reading of Andre, and now of Hawthorne, some pattern for me, some territory I wanted to be a part of.

•

I pored over political science books for a third course called *Politics of Developing Nations*—I was taking the three courses altogether. The politics course was taught by a brilliant professor, Dr. Kenneth Wiles, one of the most demanding and informative professors I'd encountered. He had an ability, in his lectures, to make you see the sweep of current history—and how it related to ancient history—before you. In Haseltine Hall, a nineteenth-century building with tall, ornate ceilings, Professor Wiles paced before us, tossing a stick of chalk from hand to hand. We were discussing political movements in the world; in Syria, Hafez Al-Assad was purging the city of Harran of the Muslim Brotherhood; in South Africa, twenty-two MPs had delivered a no-confidence vote in P.W. Botha, the white minority president, and that regime was beginning to disintegrate. In Poland, the communist government was cracking down on a union movement called Solidarity. I would walk out of class still in deep conversation with the other students. The Polish situation, in particular, had my attention: at home, my father and I watched the television pictures of communist oppression with a deepening sense of anger—Dad had been imprisoned during the communist coup in Czechoslovakia of 1948-49; he had witnessed, on American television in 1968, the crushing of the Prague Spring. We still had family there, and the Polish situation was a harsh reminder of the horrors of communist rule.

•

Sometimes when I was working in the library, I saw Andre coming over Tupelo bridge, smoking a cigarette thoughtfully, walking his huge golden Labrador, Luke. I would put my books and papers neatly aside—they were safe there—and go outside and join the two of them. Andre would smile when he saw me. He was always welcoming.

"Hey, man."

"Hey, Andre."

"Doing some homework?"

"Some poly-sci stuff."

"He's a good man, Ken," Andre said. "Serious guy."

"He's pretty exacting," I said. "He seems to care a lot about us, though, and you can ask him anything and he'll take the time to explain it to you."

"You'll earn your grade in there."

"I like the subject."

"What is it about it you like?"

"I always feel like countries are similar to human beings, the way they maneuver around each other," I said. "I did a lot of political science up at my last school in New Hampshire."

"You have the interest because of your family history—is that why? Didn't you tell me your Dad was in Europe fighting Nazis during the war?"

"He worked with the Resistance against them when he was a teenager," I said. "In Czechoslovakia. After the war, he skied for the national team and when the communists started to take over, they wanted him to preach communism to the kids there. He said he wouldn't do it and they thought he was working against them and they put him in jail."

"My God. How long did that go on?"

"About eight months. They sent him through five different prisons. He went through some terrible stuff. But he stuck to his story of the truth, that he was innocent, no matter what they did—"

Andre's profile was grim. "How did he get out?"

"It was during a paranoid time—it was a couple of years before the Slansky trials—"

"—I remember them—"

"Dad was in the same prison, in Prague; it's called Pankrác. It used to be a Nazi prison once, also. When the communists took over some of the authorities were for Stalin, some were against. Somebody finally believed that Dad was innocent, and he was kind of freakishly released in the middle of all that power struggle."

"Did he escape from the country then?"

"He worked for the Underground for a while. He smuggled some of the Democratic government ministers to freedom. He finally got shot in an ambush in Prague and escaped to Germany, and then he worked with American Intelligence there for a long time."

"He was a spy?"

"For about eight years."

Andre paused. "He was a warrior," he said.

"He was," I said. Pride and sorrow for my father caught up my voice a moment. Sometimes the knowledge of what Dad had gone through, particularly during his time as a political prisoner, was too much for me. I tried to stop the emotion by clearing my throat, and felt Andre quietly noticing. I said, "Dad was unhappy with what the US government was doing as we approached the Vietnam years. That's when he left the intelligence work."

"Does he talk about all of this?"

"Sometimes, when we're working together. Not a lot."

Andre was quiet a moment. We were close to the Bradford chapel now, and he tossed the cigarette high into a snowbank. He let Luke off the leash a moment, and Luke darted around and put his big snout down among the shiny ice patches significantly.

"We had General Westmoreland's daughter here during the war," Andre said. "I didn't like what her father was doing, but I always thought it must have been hell for her, around all her peers, when the information came out about how much the military was lying to the public about our body count over there."

I looked at the snow-crested buildings around us, imagining them in an autumn a decade before: leaves falling onto the roofs and, all over campus, protests like you saw in films of the nineteen-sixties and seventies, students marching with signs, fists in the air.

"Were there marches around here?" I said.

"Yes," Andre said. "Some in downtown Haverhill. A lot of us, students and staff and faculty, were in them." Luke came back and Andre put the leash on him and we went silently on the pathway: Luke tugged on Andre's arm, panting happily from his bout of freedom, his breath rising into the winter night air.

"What exactly do you and your father do?" Andre asked me.

"He's a consulting engineer," I said. "Basically, he trouble-shoots for various companies and he invents things. We also have a business building fiberglass boats—kayaks and rowing shells. We've got a place at the airport by the river."

"You're a hard-working guy," Andre said.

I shrugged. "I try to just stay on top of things," I said. I'd never considered myself hard-working, though when I'd thought about it, I guessed it was true. I liked that my new mentor had the impression I was industrious, but in truth, I thought of my life then as scattered more than anything else.

"And how's the music going?" Andre said.

"I've been trying to make an album," I said, smiling. "I'm at a few places playing solo, but most of the time I feel like kind of a glorified jukebox—"

"Why so?"

"People don't really listen in bars. You're just kind of back-ground."

"What kind of stuff do you play?"

"James Taylor, Eagles kind of stuff."

"I like Taylor," Andre said. "I'm a big Willie fan. I like Waylon, Kristofferson."

"I love the Janis Joplin version of 'Bobby McGee,'" I said. "How she sets fire to a song."

"Wasn't she something?" Andre said. "*Man,* she did a *beautiful* job."

CHAPTER SEVEN

We were both somber, then, remembering Janis Joplin and how things ended up for her. We made a loop around Academy Hall in the darkness of the building shadows. Snow was caught up in the vines of the old brick walls. We came around to the front of the campus, Denworth and Haseltine halls and the main driveway before us, cars rushing past on Route 125 below. Lights above flooded the scene, making the columns of Academy Hall bright white. Somewhere out on this great lawn, in a fall long ago, I'd sat on the grass as a kid. The memory came back to me: autumn colors in trees, a college girl taking care of me, showing me something she was drawing, getting me to draw, too. A college-aged guy had asked me to bring a flower to another college girl. Now I remembered this other girl's delighted face, her blond hair when I rambled over, feeling very important, with the flower.

We went around to the eastern side of Academy, where an old elm tree spread dramatically in an arc of diffuse light. It seemed like all these ghosts were caught up in the branches. Beyond it was the opened iron gate, the entrance to campus.

"Sometime in the early fifties," Andre told me now, "like 1954, a whole bunch of my friends invited me to go over to Shreveport to see a show called The Louisiana Hayride. It was this big thing they put on all the time near the border of Texas and Arkansas with country stars and up-and-coming singers. They wanted me to see this new guy named Elvis Presley. I thought—how could a guy with a name like 'Elvis Presley' ever be a star? I said forget it, man, I'm not gonna go see some weird-named guy."

Our laughter echoed off the buildings in the winter night. Luke looked back at us, smiling, wondering what all the fuss was about.

"That would have been something," I said. "Seeing Elvis just at the beginning like that."

•

We talked about everything on those walks. We talked about the Vietnam war, about how there was a part of Andre that wished he'd been sent there to take care of young Marines, how he'd grieved for the dead American soldiers. He told me about serving on the USS *Ranger;* how the aircraft carrier had anchored off the coast of Japan. He'd visited Hiroshima because he'd felt a spiritual duty to. He spoke of his time on the ship, of living at sea, of the men who'd been a family to him. He sometimes imitated a gunnery sergeant, a tough salt he'd loved who had a speech impediment and who called Andre "DeBooth."

I brought up student stories we'd gone over in class, and we went over them again now, their strengths and weaknesses. I said I'd been reading *Separate Flights,* that I was struck by the bravery and boldness of it, story after story; Andre thanked me, modestly, and asked what else I was reading. *The Snows of Kilimanjaro,* I told him ("I think Hemingway was a deeply sentimental man," Andre said, "much more than people realize or give him credit for"). I'd also recently read Steinbeck's *Cannery Row,* the form of which I really admired ("the *least* talented of our great writers," Andre said, "but he made more of his talent than anyone."). He spoke of writers I didn't know—Gina Berriault and Richard Yates and Tobias Wolff and Alice Munro and Nadine Gordimer ("probably our greatest living writer"). Afterward, in the library, I looked these authors up and read their work, hoping I could offer something more substantial to our discussions the next time we talked.

Though I wasn't conscious of it, I was developing for myself a kind of writer's code on these evening walks, learning Andre's instincts and work habits. When I was back in the library after, I entered the things Andre had told me into the margins of my writing notebook:

Make a routine of your writing. Show up for duty—then work slowly; always know what your characters are thinking before your pen leaves the page.

Hemingway used to do this: stop your writing when it is going well, in mid-sentence, in mid-thought; write a couple of notes in the margin if you need to remember where you are going. The next day you're right in the middle of it when you start up again. Train yourself this way, just like you would train your muscles for athletics—.

Some things I boxed in with ink because Andre had emphasized them:

You've got to love your characters. Don't talk down to them or be clever with them. You may not want to go to dinner with them, but you have to love them.

Follow what Flaubert said: always work to use the precise word.

Take the thing you love the most and cut it—you're hanging onto it because of your ego.

CHAPTER EIGHT

In these first months of knowing Andre, I was careful about speaking of the Catholic faith, which so clearly and deeply informed his work. The truth was, I just didn't know much about the subject. My father's family was Catholic, but Dad had been so disgusted with the workings of the Catholic church during the war (their aid in the escape of prominent Nazis to South America was a frequent point of discussion with him—) that I was not baptized and my parents had agreed that I should choose my own religion, if I cared to. My mother was Protestant and that is what was listed on my birth certificate, but I could count the times I'd been to any kind of church on one hand.

Now I was quietly taking note of how Andre's stories were often infused with the majesty, mystery, and sometimes the darker, twisted sides of the Catholic faith. In "If They Knew Yvonne," the fifth story in *Separate Flights,* a narrator identified only as Harry opens the piece when he is at age thirteen, learning about the sin of masturbation from the priests of his Catholic school in Louisiana. *Self-abuse,* the priests call it, and Harry struggles with his erotic fascinations, with the forms of women around him, the images of them in magazines, his need for release; in confession he admits to his "self-abuse."

The priests tell him to occupy himself with chores, with baseball—anything to avoid this mortal sin. One priest, in the confessional, tells him to "stick my finger in the flame of a candle, then imagine the eternal fire of Hell." At one point Harry is so confused, so caught between his primal passion and the rules of his church that he considers cutting off his penis, but a kind of common sense, a surge of self-survival, takes over before he mutilates himself.

Harry is blessed by the presence of an older, free-spirited sister named Janet, who calls into question the more severe aspects of their faith: she eventually becomes pregnant and moves away. Harry begins seeing, at age nineteen, a fellow college student named Yvonne, who he has sex with, and the sex eventually becomes so routine, so expected, that one night at a party, after telling his friends how he has "screwed" Yvonne upstairs, Harry feels great shame, looking at his girlfriend across the room, for his indifference to her soul. "If They Knew Yvonne" ends with a lightness, a recovery of sorts, when Janet returns to Louisiana after her marriage fails—her husband could not resist the temptation of other, younger women. Harry confesses to his sister, one hot summer night as moths flutter against the screens of their porch, his great sexual struggle from early on.

Janet says, "I know this much: too many of these celibates teach sex the way it is for them. They make it introverted, so you come out of their schools believing sex is something between you and yourself, or between you and God."

Here I was in Hawthorne's territory again—in this place where there was a division between enforced, institutionalized behavior and personal desire—a cleaving of the human soul. Institutions tore the individual from his or her own instincts. But where Hawthorne focused on the hypocrisy of the overall society, Andre examined that same dynamic by looking into his characters, moment by moment, with a high-powered microscope.

•

It was heady, being this close to someone of such artistic honesty and intensity. I knew that it was a gift, and I hung on and learned as much as I could, watching my mentor think things through as we walked; watching him teach, the example of artistic seriousness he set for everyone. I think Andre responded to my tenacity and curiosity. For a writer, he told me once, there's "no excuse for being bored." He got mad at me when I confessed that I didn't like to look up words in a dictionary midway through reading—I didn't want to interrupt the story. *Oh good,* he said. *A writer who doesn't like to look up words.* Then he thought about it and confessed that he went through a period where he did the same thing. This was typical of Andre when he offered harsh judgment: reconsideration, forgiveness, identification.

He was constantly urging me to look things up—words, concepts; he was forever asking questions of people, trying to figure out their motivations, getting to the root of their personalities. *The task of the writer is not to solve the problem,* he told me once, quoting his beloved Chekhov, *but to state the problem correctly.*

Whatever dignity I was finding in my new artistic life was kept in check by my occasional, glaring provincialism. Late one afternoon, walking beside Andre after class, I talked about a night scene I was writing in which, high in a window, a woman appeared as a silhouette. I somehow had it stuck in my mind that *silhouette* was pronounced *sil-hoot*. Andre stopped and looked at me, baffled.

"What the *fuck* is a sil-hoot?" he said.

"You know," I said. "A *sil*-hoot. Her dark shape up in the window."

Andre looked up and blinked his eyes at the sky in despair. "Joe, my God. That's a silhou*ette*." He shook his head back and forth in disbelief. "Holy shit."

I kept on doggedly following him, and fortunately, he tolerated me. For all my enthusiasm, it must have been clear to him that if he was going to make something of me, he had a long way to go.

CHAPTER NINE

In the airplane hangar, I tilted a high-volume kayak we called a Hurka *Expedition* on its end and braced it. I rolled a two-inch wide strip of fiberglass cloth over the seam where the deck joined the underside. I ran electrician's tape along the edges of the glass strip, then removed the strip and began sanding the area I'd taped off. A radio played a Police song, "Message In A Bottle," quietly beside me.

We had the basic hulls made from our molds by a fiberglass shop in Nashua, New Hampshire, then brought the boats down here for all the finishing work. I was creating what we called an "outside seam" to reinforce the craft. I used heavy, course paper first, not leaning into it—just breaking the gel-coat skin of the hull—then a lighter grade. The work on one side of the boat took about twenty minutes of thorough sanding. I cleaned up the gel-coat dust with a wet rag, and then, with a foam paintbrush and resin, I "wet out" the area I'd sanded. I was efficient at this work. The resin had a sharp smell, like chemical peanut butter. I rolled out the fiberglass cloth strip again—it stuck precisely to the resin I'd just put down—and began wetting it over with resin carefully, making sure to soak the entire texture of it. Fiberglassing was always a messy job that required a lot of cleaning of the hands with acetone and Lava soap afterward. In my head now, I planned out the morning: I would finish this side, then while it was curing I would fire up the ski tip operation and give it about an hour; then, when the outside seam I'd created was cured sufficiently I would flip the kayak over and do the outside seam on the other side. I would sand the cockpit, smoothing out the rough fiberglass edges, and vacuum out and clean the whole boat up with a clean wet rag, then dry the glass deck and carefully apply the *HURKA* black stickers and make the boat gleam with furniture polish, and then it would be ready for sale, waiting to be shipped out in a rack we'd constructed, at the end of the hangar, of two-by fours and foam. I would get these few things done before I washed up and went off to class with Andre.

This boat was one of three destined for a shop on the Gulf Coast of Florida. I remembered, now, how we'd once shipped seven kayaks to a sports shop in the south, only to hear that the boats had been burned in a warehouse fire. The shop had declared bankruptcy and we had taken the sizable loss. Later, we'd found out that the fire had been deliberately set for the insurance, and that our boats, along with a great deal of other equipment from other companies, had been sold off for pure profit. It wasn't an unusual story in those days, in the sports industry. That was the last time we'd sold anything on credit: everything we built now was sold COD—"cash on delivery."

•

I looked through the office doorway at my father. He was at his desk, making calculations, speaking in Czech to himself. Dad kept pressing on: he was always caught in his inventive world, thinking of some new angle on things. I remembered now some of the great times we'd had when I was a boy, the way he would get me involved in the joy of the inventive process. Once he invented an electronic "ski instructor" and had tested it out on me, aged nine. He'd strapped a battery pack to my chest and run wires down my arms; the wires ran down to grips like the grips of ski poles, except the top of the grips were lightbulbs. When you aligned your weight properly during a ski turn, the bulbs would light up. We'd had a ball testing it. I'd tested early parabolic skis, Kevlar sailboats, prototypes of rowing shells, Kevlar kayak paddles and oars; together we'd lit fire logs pressed into shape with sawdust and wax (a company called Duraflame beat us to that one). We'd even experimented with a small mechanical device that made pop-up ice cream cakes.

Now Dad was developing a way to take simple sawdust and combine it with resin to create various products; we had prototypes all over the hanger from the last few months—broom handles, axes, hammers, all unpainted, so that you could see clear into them—sawdust frozen chemically into form. I thought it was a brilliant application: there was so much wasted sawdust lying around lumber yards in this country, and all that material, with the right mixture of inexpensive chemicals, could be turned into profit. The idea had generated a lot of interest from a company in the Midwest called American Machinery Limited, and Dad was occasionally traveling to the AML plants in Glasgow, Kentucky and Aurora, Illinois, to consult with their engineers and lawyers. Dad's glasses were off now, and he was staring closely at the page before him, sometimes drawing something and underlining it precisely with the help of a ruler. When I saw him working so thoroughly—he worked this way on everything—

my heart would go out to him. I thought of all the violence and sadness he had seen in his life, and his creative, exacting work—his hopes for the family, how it never occurred to him to give up.

•

Through that spring of 1982, I went from the world of fiberglass boats and Dad's inventions to the quiet campus of Bradford, the clean arts center that I loved with its revolving photographs and art exhibits, up to the classroom where Andre was showing me a new way to engage my artistic instincts, my soul.

Many nights I played music in bars for money, often with my high school friend, Trice Burke; Trice had an incomparable voice—much better than mine—and a deep instinct for the blues. She loved songs by Bonnie Raitt and the group Heart. We wrote songs together that we performed. In our large high school, over a thousand students, we had taken guitars from the music room and sung for people under a stairway—even the hall monitors who were supposed to kick us out of there would come listen to us. Trice was like a sister to me. She was now a beautiful young woman: she had shimmering blond hair and white teeth and skin still dark from summer, and sometimes the ends of these bar gigs were spent fending off drunk men—a few times I had to push them back from the stage physically.

I was working on my album, steadily recording my songs, putting aside what money I could for studio time. My music was folk-bluesy; I admired Jim Croce and Gordon Lightfoot and John Denver and Jonathan Edwards. I worked in the studios with Trice and sometimes also with a powerful blues band I hired, and who became friends of mine, called The River Street Band. River Street had a large following in the area and had opened shows for big blues acts, including The James Montgomery Band; these days they were backing Cub Koda, the blues and rockabilly singer from Detroit who had penned the hit, "Smokin' In The Boy's Room," which he'd done with Brownsville Station early in his career.

I was young, without much wisdom, full of heart, aggressive when I needed to be. Most of the time that winter I wore black—black shirts and black or gray turtlenecks, black jeans. I'd been in a recent relationship which had ended in an abortion: the woman had told me she was medically unable to maintain the pregnancy, and we certainly hadn't been prepared to have children, but the experience had torn me to pieces, psychologically, and I was having trouble getting over it. It was not the kind of thing I could talk about with anybody, so it came out in what I wore, in my songs and—now—in the stories I wrote. One of my first stories for Andre's class was a piece called "Just A Few Trees," about a couple trying to salvage their relationship the night before the woman is due to have an abortion—essentially an autobiographical work.

The dark clothes were also because, in my own way, I was still mourning the death of John Lennon, who had been murdered two years before—I dressed often like Lennon did in the back picture of his album, *Double Fantasy*: ribbed black turtleneck, dark jeans. Once, when Trice and I went to see River Street perform with Cub Koda at the Channel, a rock club in south Boston, I stood while the band was on break and watched the huge television screen set near the bar; there was a video playing of John Lennon performing with Elephant's Memory at Madison Square Garden in 1973. Alex

Hurst, the harmonica player for River Street, came up next to me, his arms crossed, watching also. Alex was ten years older than me, a wizard on the harmonica. We talked about Lennon as, in round glasses and army sergeant's coat, the former Beatle performed a gritty, heavily-drummed version of "Come Together," and I said the first song I'd ever learned was the Beatles' "You've Got To Hide Your Love Away," and that I loved Lennon's voice on the Beatles' folky stuff, like "Norwegian Wood"; Alex told me his memories of how the Beatles records had moved him since he was a kid. We both agreed that a big part of the reason we'd gotten into music had been to meet John Lennon.

That same night at the Channel I asked Cub Koda, backstage, what he did when he got stuck writing songs. Cub was a wild performer onstage—he sometimes looked like a demented version of Elton John, with gaudy costumes and large dark glasses. The guy could really take command of an audience. Backstage I always found him to be an alternate personality—quiet and thoughtful. "Sometimes in that situation, I pretend I'm Elvis, man," he told me. "I pretend I'm writing a famous Elvis tune, and I'll write a verse and a chorus, and pretty soon what is coming out is me."

I began to relate the philosophy to my fiction: in the calm of the Bradford library, looking up some of those current authors Andre had suggested, I worked to internalize the music of their voices—I would sit in one of the upper cubicles on the second floor and quietly hum the syllables, the sentences—to Nadine Gordimer's stories, Tobias Wolff's stories, Gina Berriault—not pronouncing words, just humming. Then I bent with pen to page and tried to imitate these voices. I realized that you couldn't really sustain the duplication, because the voice of a story *is* the conscience of the writer, made into a march of human symbols; but what you could borrow was the authority of a great writer, and that confidence carried you more deeply into your own telling—into the river of your own mystery and heart.

CHAPTER TEN

Summer came to New England, at first slowly, with cool days that refused to release the mud and snow of spring, and then suddenly, as will happen in New England in May, with an explosion of color. The dogwoods and rhododendrons on either side of the Bradford library entrance were in full bloom, and there was the new smell of mown grass over the campus. My first semester at Bradford College was done.

And suddenly, things for my family were changing. Robert Covey, the president of American Machinery Limited, was convinced that my father's sawdust idea would become a huge industry—Dad now had developed the system so that it could be used to build playground equipment, and furniture for fast-food restaurants. Covey was a self-made man, tall, a gruff, salt-of-the-earth type; I had the impression when I met him that he and Dad would get on well. AML was beginning to fund Dad's research now, and a company lawyer kept flying in from Scottsdale, Arizona, to prepare patents with my father; finally, Covey asked Dad to move with the family permanently to the Aurora, Illinois, area, where the AML headquarters was located. Dad would become the head of research for the company.

It was of course a major decision—a hard choice for my mother and father; it would mean moving my brother Chris to a new school system, and upending everyone's lives. But it would also mean financial steadiness for the family for the first time in many years. And my mother would be going back to familiar territory: she had grown up on the North Shore of Chicago and had family and friends there.

Most students leave their families to go to college: by the fall of 1982 my family was leaving our home of seventeen years and I was staying in New England to continue with my studies. During the summer and school breaks, we agreed, I would travel to Illinois to help Dad (part of Dad's agreement with American Machinery was that they would provide working space for our boat business so that we could continue with that, as well). Otherwise, I would stay and take my classes—I was enrolled in a second fiction writing seminar with Andre, another political science course with Dr. Wiles, and a course in European literature; I was using whatever national and state scholarships and grants were available to me, and I would live, when our house sold, somewhere in the vicinity of the campus. Dad, with his new salary, would help me with the expenses for an apartment.

·

The house in Boxford sold then very close to the end of summer and was to be vacated in October, and I lived in it for a final few weeks. I couldn't believe I was leaving the place: it was completely empty now. My parents had done all the things realtors tell you to do—paid for sandblasting and urethaning of the floors, and they'd had the fireplace repaired and the walls painted. The old garrison looked like a glossed-over version of the house I'd grown up in. Everywhere I walked, my footsteps sounded like gunshots. I slept on a foam mattress in the guest room—one of the few rooms with wall-to-wall carpet. The familiar night shadows angled through the house, and there was the sound of the stream out back, amplified through this empty space. On my final morning, I woke to a crisp fall day, rolled up the mattress, showered, and packed the few kitchen utensils I had and my supplies and loaded all of it into the Chevy. I took a last look around. I drove out and by Witch Hollow Farm, then down past the center store, by the Indian, by the open fields of corn near Hoveys Pond, I once rode motorcycles there with friends. Main Street gave way to Kingsbury in Bradford, and in twenty minutes I was turning into the gates of Bradford College.

It was a bright autumn on campus. There was a hum in the air, the sun bright overhead. Dragonflies stitched over the black of Tupelo Pond. The college pathways were crowded with students and there was a sense of newness and possibility everywhere.

In the art gallery, a professional photographer had a showing of infrared work he'd shot in Paris—monuments and gardens that seemed to glow with secret energy. The photographer had a placard up explaining that infrared photography caught invisible light that was just beyond the spectrum of human vision. Here was the Eiffel Tower shot from a nearby park, trees in the foreground white, ecstatic. Here were shimmering white lions at the end of a wide balustrade, and a couple walking down a Parisian boulevard, unaware of the magical light that surrounded them from trees and buildings. Each day I went to my classes, I looked at a few of the infrared photographs closely. I stepped up the winding stairs and attended a literature class, then my workshop. Then I went outside after a day of study and, even in the New England gloaming, I felt the same energy as I'd seen in the photographer's work, some anticipatory brightness just hidden from view. I was in my own Paris at Bradford College.

·

I worked to establish a routine now, in this new fall, even while I missed my family, and even while I worried about how things would go for them. Something in me, I think, sensed that my father's situation was precarious, though there was nothing logical to base this on. I reassured myself: Dad had a solid and sizable paycheck now, and Mom was substituting at various high schools in French and Spanish, and tutoring at home—she excelled at being a teacher of languages, and over the next few years she would collect some four hundred students to work with. Chris had a rocky start in his first weeks at St. Charles Middle School: he'd had a rough time being accepted by some of his new peers (there were always cruel kids to contend with in such situations, and he'd run up against some of them—it enraged me) but now he'd found some good friends and things were getting better. I kept note, especially, of what was happening with Chris, and tried to talk with him often on the phone and assure him that all would be well.

·

The students at Bradford were by and large serious, intent on their learning; this whole north shore *area* of Boston seemed serious, resolved, enmeshed with the fast clip of the suburban and urban landscapes. I had my walks and deep discussions with Andre, and I continued playing my gigs at night—I was incorporating my musical and factory life into my fiction: my stories were now populated with musicians and blue-collar workers, people I'd known and lived and worked with. Andre reminded me frequently—nothing was lost on a writer.

And I took a lover: she was an adult student at the school, thirty-two, dark-haired, exquisite-looking, troubled. Married to a prominent member of the Haverhill community with whom she had not had sexual relations in seven years, she told me—her husband was often on long trips to San Francisco, or San Juan, where he took male lovers and wrote to his wife the details of these liaisons. I saw some of these strange, explicit letters. Later I would realize that the husband most likely knew about me and other lovers of hers, that this was some sort of arrangement between them, but for reasons of propriety the couple kept their secrets. I was swept, rather blindly, into the erotically charged situation. I met my lover in an apartment that her husband rented for her, one town over from Haverhill—it was in a building of stone walls and deep carpets; my lover had a lavish kitchen and a living room with a tall ceiling and a closet filled with dresses that she wore to her husband's important functions. There was a square, pale block of light from the bedroom window: the window gave view to a small, lit central courtyard. In the late fall the glass frosted over into a pattern of geometric angels before that pale light; it made me feel as though I'd reached the end of the earth somehow, that I was way out beyond where I'd expected to go.

CHAPTER ELEVEN

In observing my mentor, I began to understand some of the psychological strain, the ability to become an emotional chameleon that one had to have to earn a living and create art simultaneously. Teaching was an external exercise; writing a deep, internal meditation, and Andre swung like a pendulum between the two. I saw how he thought about things, how he approached various teaching scenarios, and I imagined myself more and more in his place, doing a job like his. In class, I sat usually to his left, and witnessed his deft handling of egos, talents, and the various, difficult personality problems that each teacher must navigate. He was a bit like a conductor of a symphony, I realized: he balanced the psychologies of the class like they were instruments. He was highly tuned to the struggles of his students.

There was a woman in our workshop who had a beautiful Puerto-Rican name: Valeria. One day, when we were reviewing her story, Valeria weathered the commentary with little expression on her face, looking down at the manuscript that she had just read aloud, reserved—contained, making notes. She always wore a coat in class, perhaps to hide her weight. She was very beautiful but gave no indication, ever, that she realized it. I thought she had insecurities that restricted her in the physical world, but on the page she could sing: she was so talented that her work was beyond the understanding of most of her classmates. Andre was intent on encouraging her.

How much of a reaction, I could see him wondering, was she having to the brash thing just said by the student named Kevin, leaning against the wall, about her story? Kevin had explained, casually, that a paragraph in Valeria's piece was confusing, that he didn't know what it meant—that perhaps she needed to think of how she would have expressed it in English 101, go back to the basics. It was a dig, a moment of Kevin's jealousy rising, but it was couched in an attitude of helpful suggestion. Andre dimmed Kevin's victory by taking him down a peg: "We're sorry, Kevin, that we can't all reach your lofty standards." Everyone laughed and Kevin smiled, leaning there against the shine of the water, and Valeria tilted her head down just the slightest bit, and colored, and wrote her notes a little more fiercely. Andre's sarcasm—a rarity for him—showed how much he was disturbed by Valeria's situation.

How to handle this for her? *A brief word of confidence*—I imagined him thinking—*said after class, might do the trick, or you could ask her to walk with you to the snack bar, to talk a little more about her story and her talent, make her aware that your faith in her prose transcends any rough thing said to her in class.*

And what about brash Kevin, how was he to be handled? He would have to be dealt with, too. There was talent in him, but he was a lazy sort and had been using the class as a waste ground for his emotional problems, and in the process interrupting the education the others should have been getting. *You could come down hard on him when the time was right in front of everyone—use a situation expressly for this purpose; sometimes it is necessary for the others to see such a student put in his place. But you don't want the students to think you've had an overreaction, which is what will happen if you let the kid get under your skin. So perhaps a straight, one-on-one discussion sometime this week about respecting his peers, letting him know that you're on to what he is doing emotionally? Perhaps that would make him think about what he is doing?*

Andre's face was flushed, his mouth closed in a firm line as he watched Kevin, then Valeria.

•

Kevin Morton's uncle was a famous crime writer. Kevin assumed because of this connection that the mantle of greatness had been passed to him, also. He was cocky, unenterprising. On the next day he was due to read, he brought in a one-sentence story—something, if I remember correctly, about an old man with glasses looking through a passenger window in a car at a younger woman in another car.

"That's it?" Andre said.

"That's it," Kevin said, proudly, smiling. "That's the whole story." He was leaning back against a vertical cement column again, his figure breaking the window light. He leaned that way so much, and had such an air of arrogance, that sometimes I wanted to go over there, pull on one of his chair legs.

There was quiet in the class. What Kevin had done hadn't been done before. It defied Andre's rule of producing at least five pages per week. What to make of it?

"That's profound," one of the female students said, uneasily, and at this recognition of his genius the writer smiled more broadly. He had dreamed up the idea of the one-sentence story to camouflage his laziness—he was unprepared for class and had whipped out the sentence probably just moments before coming to Seminar D—and now a pretty girl was calling him a genius to boot.

“That’s not profound,” Andre said. “That’s Kevin being an asshole.”

After class, Kevin, offended, decided to assert his dignity with his professor. They had stopped in front of the library and, from the snack bar windows, the rest of us saw the two of them standing very close, angry, their breaths rising. Sometimes their arms gestured. The sky above them was low and gray. I felt sorry for my mentor then, having it as a part of his job to deal with such juvenile stupidity. Sometimes, I thought, teaching certain wealthy kids in a college like this must have seemed, to Andre, like an exalted form of babysitting.

CHAPTER TWELVE

Peggy Rambach was twenty-two years younger than Andre. They met when she worked at David R. Godine, Andre's publisher in Boston; now she taught literature and writing courses at the college. She reminded me of a young Carol King in looks—she had the tawny hair and wise eyes; she often had a sardonic grin when she was listening to you and was quick to laugh, especially at male boorishness—the kind of banter that Andre and I engaged in sometimes when I walked to pick him up at their home before class. Usually, when I arrived, and Peggy and Cadence were there, the atmosphere was boisterous, but on this late October day, as I got to the door and Peggy greeted me, I could sense something somber in the home. Cadence was riding on Peggy's hip, with her tangled strawberry hair and wide, staring eyes, looking as though she'd just woken.

"Be with you in a minute, buddy," Andre said from the library, just a few steps above. Peggy looked at me and said, quietly, "He's having an emotional time with a story he's writing."

Andre described it to me as we walked. "I've been writing about this woman named Rose," he said. "She's married to this fucking guy—this child abuser. This morning he picked up their six-year-old boy and threw him into a wall and broke his arm."

Peggy had told me on the landing, quietly, as I waited, that immediately after writing Andre had been weeping. What struck me, at this moment as we walked, was Andre's complete surprise at his character's actions. He talked about this often: that at the start of a story he would have loose plans for about three scenes, and then the characters began to guide the work and he had no real sense of where things were going. In this story, we meet Rose through the eyes of an unnamed narrator, in a bar called Timmy's in Haverhill. Rose is an older woman at this point, and people guess at her history: she is quiet about her past. But on this winter night, she opens up to the narrator and tells him her story. Of her marriage to Jim Cormier, a construction worker, a man who, frustrated with his lack of mobility, outwitted by the circumstances of his life, becomes abusive to Rose and their three children, a boy and two daughters. With his violence, Cormier slowly breaks down the spirit of Rose, his family. One night, Jim Cormier throws the boy against a wall and breaks his arm. Rose, in a fury, takes the boy to the car to get him to the hospital; she looks up at the apartment to realize that her husband has set their home on fire with the two girls inside. She clubs him over the head with a gas can as he is trying to escape the building; then she runs to her girls, saving them by dousing blankets in the shower, wrapping her daughters, and running with them through the flames.

". . .*It's the only thing I ever did,*" Rose tells the narrator, on this night in her older age, "*in my whole fucking life. The only thing I ever did that was worth a shit.*" But the narrator, in looking at the totality of Rose's existence, sees her much differently; he sees her as resilient, a survivor, redeemed. *I see her young and strong and swift, wrapping the soaked blankets around her little girls, and hugging them to her, and running and spinning and running through the living room, on that summer night when she was touched and blessed by flames.*

"Rose" would become one of Andre's great masterpieces: a song about the fragility and resistance of the human spirit, and about redemption and the inner, secret strength Andre believed all of us have—a primary theme in much of his work. Now as we walked, Andre was midway through his creation, grieving, the story unfinished and the scene of the abused child still deeply alive in him. The trees, blazing with color, swayed and groaned over Tupelo Pond with the wind, and the breeze ruffled the black surface of the water. The pond, at the edges, was full of leaves that were crystalized with a first frost. We went over the bridge talking, Andre slowly making the transition from writer to teacher.

CHAPTER THIRTEEN

Mid-November: my last night of three at Mill One, an old-time bar on Washington Street in Haverhill. Near midnight. I played in the dining area, set up with a borrowed Shure amplification system, and with my booming Guild F-50; the Guild was my constant companion in those days. I'd worked a summer of extra jobs for it a few years back. Three women watched me together from a booth, and some other stragglers came in occasionally, but the real Haverhill crowd was up at the bar, laughing, drunk, watching the Patriots on a television that played silently over the bartender's head. I sang through "Everybody Knows Her," by Jonathan Edwards, and Crosby, Stills and Nash's "Just A Song Before I Go." I played the Eagles' "Take It Easy" and "Tequila Sunrise." The women nodded their heads to the songs, but no one else paid attention. One of the women came up and asked for my phone number, the others laughing and telling her she was such a bad bitch, breaking into drunken hysterics. They looked like housewives having a reunion, perhaps happy to get away from their men for a while. I said no, no, that's fine, and went to my guitar case and gave her a business card I'd had made up, smiling. At the end of the evening another woman, drunk, black hose torn, threaded her way through the booths and sat right on the stage beside me; she sang the last songs with me, ending with John Denver's "Leaving on a Jet Plane," word for word. She was crying, her mascara running. I wondered what had happened to her.

I asked if she was okay, was there anything I could do? She nodded that she was all right and then for a moment couldn't seem to speak. The women in the booth drifted out, waving so long; the booths were empty then and the woman with the torn hose stood as I went to put my guitar away. She said, "So long, I loved your playing," and held my arm and squeezed my hand a moment and went into the night. I watched her go and wondered if I should have insisted that she sit and tell me what the trouble was. The drunks were shouting up by the bar, some being herded out slowly by the bouncers. The owner, smiling, came to me and brought an envelope—he was paying me for my three nights.

"I wish I'd brought in more business for you," I said.

"It's fine, you did fine," he said. We both knew it wasn't true. He was a middle-aged guy, his hair dyed black and starting to thin; he was a trusting sort. For some reason, he'd wanted the live music, the single guitar player. Maybe he just wanted it as kind of an image to greet people with when they came in. But it was not that kind of place, and as much as I liked the guy, I wasn't going to do it again. Something in me was tired of using music this way, just to make a few dollars a night.

Outside, I walked quickly, firmly, to the Chevy. I loaded the Shure system first—speakers and mic stand and microphones and mixer—into the back. This part of Washington Street wasn't all that safe at this hour, and lights were out above, over the sidewalk, so I worked in shadows; I locked the car and went back and got my guitar and said goodnight to everyone.

When I came out again, a large truck was just coming down Washington from LaFayette Square: its lights went over the buildings and, high to my right, washed over the deeply etched numbers in one wall: *1852*. Across the street, on the shore of the Merrimack, were the remains of the last mills of Haverhill, now bars and shops and some abandoned buildings; at night, I always felt the ghosts of the workers here, how they must have lived in tenements on the street, come in crowds down this sidewalk in their early mornings one hundred years before, facing long, grindingly-difficult days in the woolen mills, the shoemaking factories, the tanneries.

I unlocked the car again and put the Guild in and motored over the Vietnam Veterans' Bridge, the dark Merrimack below me. I thought about that poor woman sitting on the stage—was she a prostitute? Probably. I'd heard somewhere that upward of one hundred prostitutes were working in Haverhill now. Where did she go—where did she rest tonight? I imagined her trying to sleep with whatever discord was within her, whatever had happened to her, whoever had assaulted her spirit. At least, I thought, if my music wasn't good for anything else tonight, it had helped her—maybe? Brought some peace to her? I hoped so.

I got on Route 495 South toward Methuen and Lawrence, and soon I was going down the incline of Route 35, watching before me the old smokestacks of the Lawrence mills rise in the night.

CHAPTER FOURTEEN

I'd called Paul Garnier, a childhood friend and neighbor, when it had come time to search for an apartment. As kids, Paul and I had shot our BB and pellet guns in the gravel pit behind our neighborhood, and played football and basketball and baseball together, and waited hundreds of mornings with the other neighborhood kids for our old yellow bus to come rumbling up, doors hissing open. Paul's large Catholic family was originally from the Lawrence area and I knew he'd have ideas about inexpensive places to live. He was a big guy, a former high school wrestler, and he was now working as a jail guard at the Lawrence prison. An apartment was available in the same complex he lived in, he told me, in Methuen on the Lawrence line. He gave me the number of the management company. The complex was a three-story, U-shaped set of cheap places that bordered the Merrimack River, and the apartment I took was on the first floor, partially submerged into the ground. I was right across the courtyard from Paul and sometimes we saluted each other across that space.

I remember the buildings as brick, whitewashed, built perhaps in the 1960s. The apartments had cheap carpets and walls painted in semi-gloss eggshell-white, and the grounds were always littered with cigarettes and newspapers. You could walk down from the parking lot a few feet to a railroad bed with abandoned tracks and the Merrimack was right there, dark and brooding, sliding through that industrial area. Phone lines stretched over the tracks, the smokestacks and mills across the water rising out of the nineteenth century.

For furniture, I had a well-used, Naugahyde couch that had belonged to my parents, duct-taped in places. I had a folding card table to eat on with two fold-out chairs; for a bed, I put down four cinder blocks with plywood over it, and a foam mattress on top. A small stereo sat on my bedroom floor and there was another card table in there with my IBM Selectric—Dad had given me the typewriter. We'd had it for years at our Newburyport shop and then at the airplane hangar. I sat in a plastic garden chair as I wrote and typed. I wrote in longhand first, in record books, like my mentor, then set to work on the Selectric. Sometimes there was music thumping down from the apartment upstairs, something that made me crazy, and I would go up and ask for quiet; the tenant there was also the manager of the apartment complex and occasionally difficult to deal with, and I couldn't believe I had to keep asking. Looking back, I'm sure my typing didn't thrill him, either. I was on that Selectric all the time.

The greater Lawrence area was crowded, a collage of brick, cement, and tar, filled with the old textile mills. Many of the buildings were fading, hollow brick shells, their walls glaring with graffiti. Old steel bridges crisscrossed the Merrimack River. The running joke in those days was that so many cars had been disposed of in the Merrimack to cheat insurance companies that you could pretend you were Jesus and walk across the water. It wasn't unusual, in that area, to see Puerto-Rican or Black gangs; I came back from Bradford one evening to see a Puerto-Rican gang chasing a group of Black teenagers down the street with pipes, police cars with their sirens swiftly howling behind.

Some nights I drove to Andover, to the expensive stone building. I have a memory of my lover and I sitting on her couch, her legs across my lap. She was reading, a soft lamp over her left shoulder. I was reading, probably then Richard Yates' *Liars in Love.* We'd been in bed: we'd put our clothes back on, we were pleasantly disheveled. I couldn't believe how good-looking this woman was, her profile against the light, the smoothness of her legs. The light shone through her fingers, the paper; she put the book on the end table and reached there for some letters that were bound with a rubber band. She slipped one letter out and the light revealed the heavy slant of her husband's handwriting. She passed pages to me after she read them over—the letter described a gay bath house in San Francisco, where her husband was visiting—I skimmed through the explicit sections. At the end, he spoke of his concern for a new disease, new cases in Los Angeles among gay men. The disease was still shrouded in mystery: it was primarily spread by sexual contact and attacked the immune system.

When I was finished, I handed the pages back. My lover took the bundle of letters, unwrapped the rubber band from around them, fit the newest one into the bundle and snapped the rubber band back over all of it. She got up and put the letters in a desk drawer. "Doesn't hurt to hold onto these," she said. "A woman never knows when this kind of evidence might come in handy."

•

There was a rehearsal loft on Broadway in Lawrence where Trice and I sometimes met The River Street Band to go over songs. It was a tight space, full of musical equipment, bright, intense, sweaty. I didn't smoke grass or drink, but the band often lit up and sometimes, when I left, I was sailing just from the second-hand smoke. I'd had enough of drugs during some hospitalizations as a youngster—I didn't see the sense in taking them recreationally, but these rehearsals usually included the thick marijuana haze and a liberal use of Wild Irish Rose, which the band called, affectionately, *Wild I.* These guys were tremendous musicians and I looked up to them: it only occurred to me now, seeing them in their home environment, that some of them probably had serious, enduring troubles with alcohol and drugs.

The prison where Paul worked was full of guys who'd fought on the Lawrence streets, a holding pen for men awaiting trial. I went there on a couple of occasions to drop off mail for Paul; he was in a cage, and behind him, beyond a wall of steel screening, was the exercise area where the prisoners walked. I slid Paul his letters through a metal slot: this was in a dank part of the old building and the barred windows were high, greasy. The prisoners walked around in their blue prison outfits, smoking cigarettes. When they wanted something, it would be handed to them through another metal slot.

•

When I'd just moved in, Paul and I often got together for dinner—usually something revolving around cheeseburger Hamburger Helper—to us, a luxury—and Paul would tell me about the various cases they had in the prison—a hardcore collection of armed robbers and murderers. Some of the jail guards were rough characters, too. At one point, for a period of about two weeks, a prison guard whose wife had thrown him out of the house stayed at Paul's apartment. I don't know if the man ever took a shower. Big and imposing as Paul could be, he had always been, deep down, a good-natured guy and it seemed to me that his generosity was being taken advantage of. One night, when I stopped there to drop off a book Paul had lent me, the man, whose name was Hector, was sitting on Paul's couch with the phone beside him. Hector had taken off his shoes and socks and his feet were up on the coffee table and the place reeked. He was calling a prostitute who, apparently, regularly serviced him.

"Hey, Joe," he said, looking up at me. "You want a blow job, too? Marielle will take care of you, no problem." It was like he was putting together an order for take-out food.

I shook my head no and told Paul quietly I was heading out. I do not know how Paul put a stop to what was happening: I suspect that was the night he drew a line in the sand and finally threw the guy out. Outside, it had snowed a little, and the snow looked dirty instantly wherever it settled—such was the effect that apartment complex seemed to have on anything new. I walked between the buildings, nauseated, thinking of that poor woman's head in that man's lap.

It was nearly winter then. More and more I made the drive from the industrial jungle of the Lawrence area up 495 to Bradford, even on days I didn't have classes, and spent time on the campus. I'd bring a bagged dinner or get a meal at the snack bar and then I'd write on the long tables beneath the library lights, late into the evenings, as the snow fell outside. The college became my refuge, more my home than the apartment by the train tracks.

CHAPTER FIFTEEN

I spoke of the prostitutes with Andre, one evening after a winter rain had fallen. He had just been walking, without Luke this time, and I'd seen him coming over the bridge. He was wearing the Akubra hat and a long oilcloth jacket that he often wore in the rain and cold.

"I keep having nightmares about that woman's head in that man's lap," I said. "She must be caught in some goddamned spiral of drugs or something, to keep having to live that way."

"Goddamn. That's fucking *awful,*" Andre said. He had this way, when he saw how the world affected me, of repeating the information with a similar emotion, letting me know I wasn't going through it alone. "A lot of these lives are lived in *horror,*" he told me. "All fucked up with drugs and sad decisions. And scavengers taking advantage."

How did people survive, living lives like that? we said, our breaths rising. Students passed us, nodding hello. Inside Hemingway, students were bent to the tables behind the warm glass, preparing for finals. The early winter rain had frozen on the valerian shrubs here, the stalks glazed black and clear in the library lights. The chapel and the snack bar were coated with ice and snow. I told Andre about the woman who had sat on stage with me, and how disturbed I was, imagining her days and nights, the demons she had to live with.

"It's like in this Chekhov novella I just read," I said. "*A Case of Nerves*—"

"That's a *powerful* story," Andre said. "Sometimes it is translated as 'A Nervous Breakdown'—"

"—where this character completely self-destructs in his worry for prostitutes in Moscow?—he goes there with a couple of friends—"

We spoke of it: Chekhov's Vassilyev, a law student, walking with two friends on a winter night in the 1880s. Vassilyev's companions are fellow students, and he is trying to adopt their jolly mood: they are all going to cruise through the brothels of the city. But once there, in the S. Street district, Vassilyev has a great struggle with his conscience—he cannot separate himself from the idea that these women who are being used for sex, who are sometimes physically slapped around, are human beings, due the same dignity as everyone else. His internal struggle leads to a mental breakdown.

"Vassilyev is the only one of the bunch who sees what is happening on a human level," Andre said, as we repeated the story to each other this night. "And he is the one, by society's standards, who slips into madness. Chekhov is telling us: *to be considered sane we must participate in the indifference of the world.* You can get overwhelmed—condemned as impractical—if you care too much. One thing that always strikes me is this phrase people use when they see something immoral or unjust and don't want to deal with it. *I don't want to get involved.* Thing is, once you say that, you already *are* involved."

I nodded at how true this was. I said: "What I don't get, and I guess I never will, is how you can use the flesh of someone else for your own fantasy."

"That's a rough fucking thing," Andre said. "That poor fucking woman."

We walked together in that dark night, Andre trying to calm me down. We spoke of our love and admiration for Chekhov; we went over particular stories. That was the night, too, that we spoke in depth about Faulkner—I mentioned *As I Lay Dying* and *The Wild Palms,* and Andre wanted me to read *The Bear;* we talked about a student in the workshop who was clearly influenced by Faulkner's voice—it sounded, at points, like she was just trying to imitate him.

"You have to be very careful reading him if you are in the middle of writing a story," Andre told me. "His voice is so compelling that you can get caught up in the music of it and start to mimic him."

We'd made a circle of the campus, and we were back up to the valerian shrubs. Andre asked me how I would describe them. The wind was blowing lightly and the shoots brushed against each other and I said *clicking* and *iced* and he said *translucent*, *glass*, *glowing in the light*, and I was better now, after walking and talking with my friend and mentor.

•

And then it was December, an afternoon in the Bradford College bookstore—a small shop just behind the art gallery—Andre and I wandering through, the two of us lost in the rows and rows of books. In addition to the glossy course texts the place was always stocked with good literature, and though I couldn't afford any of the anthologies or collections or novels, I could get completely absorbed there in my off-hours. I was into the pages of an anthology called *A World of Great Stories,* selected and edited by Hiram Haydn and John Cournos: you could travel the world of modern fiction with this book, with authors from Europe, the United States, New Zealand, China and Korea and India and Brazil. Some names I recognized; most I didn't. I'd always loved anthologies of fiction; leafing through, seeing the different ways authors made you fall into their stories. I was reading the beginning lines of Jean-Paul Sartre's "The Wall."

"You should get it, buddy," Andre said, at my side now.

I made some quick calculations. I would have liked to impress my mentor with a demonstration of how I could spontaneously come up with the money for art, then decided against the falsity. I thought of Christmas coming, presents I wanted to get for my family, money I'd saved for studio time, an electric bill looming. I shook my head.

"I'd like to get it," I told Andre honestly, "but I'll wait, see if maybe they have it in the library."

I put the book back and glanced at some other books, felt Andre looking at me, felt my face burn with shame. I was always ashamed at my lack of money. Andre let me have my dignity, and quietly went back to looking at some books himself.

But the next day, as he came into class in Seminar D, he slid the book across the table to me. *For Joe,* he had inscribed it, *because he's hesitant; but a good writer too—Andre. 7 Dec 82.*

CHAPTER SIXTEEN

The last time I'd recorded with The River Street Band, things had turned into a fiasco. We'd been working in a converted barn in the country—an inexpensive, sixteen-track studio just outside Haverhill. It had been in the early fall, and clear to me that the session would have to be my last for a while: I just couldn't scrape the money together anymore to continue with my project. I hadn't ever paid the band much: they'd done the sessions mostly because they were good guys—the whole band had taken only a few hundred dollars at a shot, helping me out. Eric Stine, the big, good-natured lead guitar player of the group, was unusually, raging drunk this day and notes he could normally ace were an unending chore; we did take after take and Eric apologized after each one: always a note was off, or he was off on his timing. Usually, these guys didn't drink when they were recording, and Vinny Morales, the seasoned bass player of the group, came up to me with Alex Hurst to apologize for the whole thing, and they told me they shouldn't take any money from me. I don't remember if I paid them or not; I probably insisted on it. We finally got something that approximated a finished song. But that session—I still have the tape, boxed up in a closet—was a howling mess.

Eric soon went into a rehabilitation facility, brought there after a bout with alcohol poisoning, and the band, for a time, fell apart. It was tough to see: they could have easily been an important national act. Like so many gifted musicians before them, they had sabotaged their own success.

In January, Paul Garnier came over to my apartment one night after work, still in his dark-blue guard uniform, to ask if I'd heard the news about the River Street drummer, Reggie Moore. Reggie was the newest guy in the band and I'd known him only about a year; he was a big black guy, powerful on the drums, soft-spoken; I'd always thought of him as a gentle giant.

"He's up on murder charges."

"Murder?" I was at the stove, putting together some cheeseburger Hamburger Helper, and I turned to Paul. "How is that *possible?*"

"Looks like he strangled a woman."

Her name was Courtney Bates, and the story was that she owed Reggie money for cocaine she was buying from him. She'd been found in her apartment in Lawrence earlier that month, half-naked, in a bathtub. Her wrists were bound behind her back and lashed to her ankles. She had been strangled with a tightly knotted scarf. Her apartment was in chaos, the telephone line cut. I couldn't imagine the guy I knew doing it, but I had to admit I didn't know him well. Reggie went to prison, convicted of second-degree murder: until his death, twenty-six years later, he maintained his innocence. On that January night when Paul told me about it, Paul also said that Reggie wanted me to visit him in prison. I never did.

There are moments when you realize you are at an end of things. I was at the end of doing my music the way I was doing it. I'd felt it on that night, two months before, after playing at Mill One where hardly anyone listened. I'd felt it in the chaotic recording session. I felt it now, listening to Paul tell me about the Reggie Moore case as we sat at the kitchen table. I imagined the other band members, how they would take it—they would hide their shock at the situation with fast quips, tough Massachusetts boys. Because Reggie had been the most recent member of River Street, they would say they'd never really known him. They'd been talking about putting the band together again. But all of this, the drugs, the drinking, the murder, would gather like something twisted and dark from within them that they wouldn't be able to overcome. I looked out the window as Paul spoke. Snow was coming down, burying the courtyard, the train tracks by the river, glazing the telephone lines white. I couldn't believe all that had happened in such a brief period.

•

It was shortly after all this that my father wrote to tell me that Robert Covey, the president of American Machinery Limited, had been diagnosed with pancreatic cancer. I was just about to start the spring semester at Bradford. I held the letter in my living room, feeling like I was rising above myself as the news and all its implications hit me.

Robert Covey was dead within two weeks. The company would now be run by his four children, the oldest of whom quickly bought himself a new, silver Mercedes C123 to drive into the president's parking spot at work. Other misguided decisions swiftly followed, including that Dad's sawdust technology was not a direction the company would continue with. Dad and Robert Covey had been right about the technology: other companies picked up the idea and put it into production, and today I see sawdust pressed into shape to make tables and chairs at fast food places, playground equipment, tools, even guitars. But Covey's offspring—my sense, in meeting them, was that they were nice enough but a pampered group—couldn't be counted on to carry on his vision. I'm not sure how long it took for them to run their father's company aground, but today American Machinery, founded in 1975, no longer exists.

In a letter Dad wrote me, soon after Covey's death, he told me not to worry: he had a severance package that would last into the summer, and he could go back to the boat and consulting businesses full-time. I put on my leather coat and slipped the letter in the inner pocket and went out to walk by the train tracks. Now, I thought, pacing and trying to work this all through on a flat winter day, Dad was in a part of the country that was new, and even though there were national contacts he could rely on, a lot of this would be like beginning again, and he was fifty-eight years old. I felt a cold fear go through me.

The mills across the river were a solid block of abandoned brick walls against the snow. My dream of making an album was a set of expensive tapes, sitting in my apartment—what a silly dream I'd had! My family's situation needed a lot of thought, and I would have to help as much as possible when I got back to Illinois in May. I debated leaving college right away, but I didn't want to give up the new semester: at least I could get through these few months. And Dad would never have gone for it, would have known that I was quitting now because of his misfortune. That would hurt him more than anything else I could do. What I had, for the time being, was this college in Haverhill, and a teacher who had faith in me.

Somewhere around this time I also had the good sense to get out of my entanglements with the older lover. Life had gotten too serious to allow myself to be involved in someone else's confusing, dark games.

PART TWO

CHAPTER SEVENTEEN

Mackie's Bar, sitting directly on Main Street in Bradford, looked, that March, like a dilapidated gray shack—it stood out for its decrepitude even in that run-down neighborhood. It was surrounded by a row of old shops behind glass windows and a well-used McDonald's, and across the street, there was a car dealership with these little triangular flags on a line, and a roast beef joint, and a small mall with a pizza shop and a garish video store. But Mackie's was the worst of it and as I walked there now with Andre and a group of students, I could see the roof of the place on its simple slant, the tar paper whitening.

The snow was falling through this late afternoon, and we filed into a loud room with lots of voices and rock music; there was a simple, shining bar, now crowded with elbows and glassy-eyed faces and cigarettes in fingers and hands holding drinks, the wall behind the bartender with shelf on shelf of dark bottles. This was the bar called "Timmy's" in Andre's fiction, where the story "Rose" and so many scenes from other stories took place. Over here to the left, near the window, there were well-worn wooden tables. We gathered around one. Andre was at home in this loud space: he'd once had a job here as a bartender to supplement his income. He took off his Red Sox jacket and Akubra hat and orders were given.

I had my normal discomfort that I do in such environments, with the constant music in the background that distracts me so much (I get so involved with listening, trying to figure out what the musicians are doing, that I can't quite concentrate on what anyone is saying). Still, I liked being here with everyone: across the table from me snow fell against a hazy window. I particularly liked the college women who had come along: there was Claire Ahlman, her blond hair slightly matted to her neck with snow, beads of wetness at her collarbone as she took off her jacket now; there was Marie Cote, from California, with her short brown hair and big, flirtatious eyes. A woman named Brooke Evans was beside me, and I'd heard that she was involved with Andre's son, Andre III, whom I'd never met. I already called him Young Andre to distinguish him from his father; Young Andre was the focus of many stories on the Bradford campus. He'd been a social worker in Colorado, a boxer, a bouncer, a bounty hunter; he'd gotten his degree in sociology in Texas. I *thought* his girlfriend was this Brooke, but I wasn't sure if they were together anymore. She'd been in the first workshop with me, brown-haired and dark-eyed, very attractive.

The drinks came and evening fell, making the street outside the window blue, giving a sense that we were all more intimately connected. I did my best to concentrate on conversations with Claire, then Marie, watching their mouths carefully because the songs were pulling at me. The women held their beers, rolling the bottles between their fingers, and spoke of a new rock group from Haverhill that was going to be performing in Boston soon, at the Channel. I thought of telling them all that had happened with River Street, then decided not to try and explain it in that noise.

With a couple of drinks in her, Marie began to tease me about my Seven-Up, to quiz me about why I wasn't a drinker, why I wasn't trying at least marijuana, or some simple drugs to help me "let loose, escape." *You're so tight, sometimes, Joe, you seem constricted. Is your whole life work?* She stared at me with those big, beautiful eyes. I had a tough time deciding if I had offended her, somehow. I didn't know her well: this was a side of her I hadn't seen.

I inevitably got asked, in drinking company, why I didn't drink or smoke grass. Was I judging people, not doing these things? They often thought so.

"I've had a lot of drugs in me for medical reasons," I said, shrugging. "It just isn't my thing."

"But if you drank a little, smoked a little weed, perhaps that would lessen your anxiety," Marie said.

Brooke leaned into the conversation. "I admire you're not doing it, Joe, if you don't want to," she said.

Marie ran a finger over the top of her Corona bottle, looked at me, considering. I thought, looking at her beauty, of how many men must have considered her opinions seriously, just for a chance for attention from her. I shook my head.

"I just went through a thing with a blues group I was working with—it involved drugs," I said. "It was pretty bad. I don't have any interest in any of it, really."

"You're a musician?" Marie said.

"I play guitar," I said.

Elton John sang in the background, and Brooke beside me said *I love these lyrics;* I heard her singing to herself, then, *Laughing like children living like lovers rolling like thunder under the covers.* I felt her arm graze against mine, and turned and looked at her brown eyes, the way they were set off by her dark knit sweater, her brown hair. It occurred to me, then, how unexciting I must have seemed to many of these college women—I didn't speak much of myself, wasn't comfortable with it, probably appeared to be just a steady, ordinary, commuting student from the area. In situations like this, I was pretty much worthless. I was comparing myself to the ghost of Young Andre; in stories I'd heard about him he seemed to have the capacity to surprise and shock, to be the life of any gathering, a wild edge about him. Eyes of women lit up when they spoke of him. If he were here, I guessed, he would have the others roaring with laughter at something irreverent, and here I was, explaining seriously why I didn't drink or do drugs. Regular Casanova.

His father, at the head of the table, was joking now with a couple of regulars, two men who were clearly glad that the college women had come in, and who raised their beers and flirted shamelessly with the girls around that end of the table. Also beside Andre was Donald Fratti, thirty-three years old, a lawyer's son who still apparently lived at home, a Bradford student in the current workshop I was in. It was a private joke with others that whenever you were in a bar with Donald Fratti you realized, at a certain point in the evening, that you were paying for all his drinks. Fratti was listening carefully now to something Andre was saying: he had a thin face and looked, to me, like a sly, warped version of Leonard Nimoy; his mustache grew long toward his cheeks, and he was in the habit of tugging on the ends as he narrowed his eyes and concentrated on his next move. You imagined, as you looked at him, how easily a cartoonist could turn him into a sinister mooch.

I left when the cacophony began to overwhelm me. I was one of the first to go, and Brooke, who had been sitting quietly by my side, asked if she could walk back toward the college with me; she lived in a dorm room in Academy Hall. She took her nearly full beer with her and we put on our coats. Outside, in the quieter, indifferent sounds of the city, Brooke told me she'd been bothered by Marie's trying to embarrass me about not doing drugs, that I shouldn't ever change just because people like Marie wanted company in their bad habits. One of the things Brooke liked about me, she said, was my independence. Marie did this often, she said—came off as all innocent and intelligent and fun to be with when she was sober, but when she was drinking or drugging this thing came out that was actually pretty vicious. I laughed and said it didn't bother me, even though it had—in truth it had bothered me a great deal. Even slightly drunk as she was, I had the feeling I probably wasn't fooling Brooke about my emotions.

The sidewalk was white with feathery snow. Brooke worked to lighten the conversation. We joked about Donald Fratti and what a crazy bar Mackie's was; our footprints were a few inches deep. We kicked at the drifts. The snow fell straight down into Brooke's hair.

I had just moved into a first-floor apartment on Cogswell Street, close to the college—it was in an old home but well-maintained and cheaper than the Methuen apartment, and there was no one playing music upstairs, so I could concentrate on my writing and songwriting. Brooke came in to see my new place—it was small, but well-cared for by the landlord, with a living room that looked out through bay windows onto the side street, now purely white, streetlamps lighting cars, everything white out there, porch stoops of other buildings, iced porch railings. I switched on the lights. There was a deep wall-to-wall rug in the room. I was embarrassed that

I had only the Naugahyde couch set up—it was against the bay window—and the two garden chairs. Brooke said it was nice, even so. Even the legs of the couch were gone at this point and so the piece sat on the floor—imagining it through Brooke's eyes I thought it probably looked pretty sad. You could see my bed—my cinderblock and foam contraption—sitting out there in the bedroom, just past the kitchen. I had my F-50 and two other guitars—an electric and a nylon-string—leaning against the living room wall here.

In the small tour of the place I gave her I joked with Brooke about the gas stove: it seemed to go out a lot and I was always worried about blowing myself up when I tried to light it. She laughed and I asked if she wanted a drink—I had orange juice and seltzer water in the old, rattling fridge, and she smiled and said no thanks and held up her unfinished beer. We sat on the couch, talking. The road was so bright outside that you could still see it clearly, even with the indoor lights on. That snow was obliterating the tracks on the sidewalk we'd made just minutes ago. It had been a couple of months since I'd stopped seeing the married woman and Brooke was acting flirtatious and that sexual hunger was in me. I watched as Brooke raised the bottle and the amber liquid smashed into her lips. She was sitting close to me, and when she lowered the bottle again, her dark eyes looked at me, holding my gaze. What was the story between her and Young Andre? I didn't know. Were they still together? She wasn't acting that way. There could be many reasons for this flirtation—what was it about, precisely? An effort to make Young Andre jealous? Perhaps not, I thought, maybe their relationship was over and this was genuine; but despite my erotic yearnings I knew suddenly it would be foolish to involve myself here, not knowing the situation, especially since it would inevitably affect the relationship with my new mentor. And Brooke was drinking: her judgment about all this might be much different tomorrow.

It took some doing to extract myself from the situation. I said I was just getting over a relationship; I wasn't ready for another. It was kind of true. I offered to walk Brooke back to Academy Hall, where she lived. But she was angry, sullen, now, her mood switching fast: she didn't want me to walk her. She put her coat on and went out, into the lights of the streetlamps, the snow coming down around her, looking back at me with some accusation, then slipping into the darkness. I was worked up, confused; I paced back and forth across the living room. I didn't like that I wasn't walking her the rest of the way, but she would make it home okay—it was just a few blocks up and the sidewalk was mostly well-lit and other college students were walking back and forth to town. I needed to think—about whether to telephone Andre and tell him to mention all this to his son, or not. If she was my girlfriend, I guessed I would want to know.

I called Andre later that evening. Better that, I thought, than for his son to hear it all from an angry Brooke—I didn't know her, really, and who knew what story she would tell? Andre told me not to worry, he thought maybe Brooke and his son had broken up.

"Did you leave early because of Marie?" Andre asked me.

"She was a little on the rude side, but I just needed some fresh air."

"I heard she was giving you shit about not getting high. You sure had a great night with the women."

"It was a little fucked up," I said.

"Don't worry about what others think of you," Andre told me. "You're your own man. Genuine people respect that. Marie's got a good heart deep down, but she's a confused kid. You just stay as you are, buddy. You're doing fine."

"Thanks, Andre," I said, pacing across that room with the phone to my ear. I kept pacing for a good while after we'd hung up, reviewing the whole thing.

CHAPTER EIGHTEEN

About a week later, I was walking alone one evening near the Bradford chapel when a guy a little older than me was suddenly beside me, asking if I was Joe Hurka. My impression as I think about Andre Dubus III now was that he was wearing dark colors like me, some kind of flannel shirt, blue and black, and jeans; he was tall and a little ragged, somehow, not really dressed for the cold. He was good-looking, his features sharp. There was something neglected though benevolent about his spirit—you sensed a clear edge in him, like he was prepared to fight for his existence, but deep down he sincerely hoped he wouldn't come to that. There was a reserve to him that I recognized as an extreme sensitivity.

He'd heard something had happened between Brooke, the girl he'd been seeing, and me; he wondered if he could hear the story from me. There was nothing threatening in his manner—just the question. I told him the truth—taking pains not to portray myself as entirely innocent; beneath the campus lights, our shadows arced as we crunched over the snowy walkways. Young Andre confirmed what I'd been thinking—that he and Brooke had hit a rough patch in their relationship, and he wasn't sure where they were at. We talked about relationships and how hard it was to make them work when they were long-distance. I said I'd just been in a strange relationship with an older, married woman—I explained it to him—that at times left my head spinning. We talked about women, and writing, and acting. Finally, he held out a hand and thanked me and, to the surprise of both of us, I think, we ended up realizing we liked each other.

Perhaps Young Andre saw in me what I sensed in him: something of a desperate need to help people we loved, to take on the weight of family difficulties. Thirty years later, reading his memoir, *Townie,* I realized how hard things had been for him and his brother, Jeb, and two sisters, Nicole and Suzanne: a childhood of uncertainty and violence in the poorer sections of Haverhill and Newburyport after their parents' divorce; a sometimes distant and contentious relationship with their father. For now, Young Andre had moved temporarily in with his Dad and Peggy, and the two of us occasionally got together there, sitting at the kitchen table, talking about authors we were reading. Young Andre was an accomplished actor, and I think at that point he still wanted to make a career of it—he'd done theater for a number of years. But there was an internal side to him—I felt it clashed somewhat with the exhibitionist I felt one had to be to act—that ran deep.

•

Young Andre and I had both stumbled simultaneously on the work of Breece DJ Pancake, the extraordinary West Virginian writer whose short stories had been primarily published in *The Atlantic Monthly,* and who had died, by suicide, four years before: Pancake had killed himself with a shotgun in 1979 at age twenty-six. His stories focused on the hardscrabble lives of people he'd known in Appalachia; the posthumous collection of his fiction, *The Stories of Breece DJ Pancake*, had been nominated for a Pulitzer Prize. We sat at the small dinner table off Andre and Peggy's kitchen, trading our favorite Pancake lines and observations; I remember my new friend speaking with deep respect for the work, late-afternoon light on the walls, behind him a painting: a Spanish town on a cliff, dark reds and browns. I said I'd been moved by the introduction to the book by James Alan McPherson, a professor of Pancake's at the University of Virginia. I knew McPherson's name from work I'd read of his in the Norton Anthology, in the class given by Russell Banks in New Hampshire.

"I love that intro, too," Young Andre said, his eyes widening. "It's like he gets right into Pancake's *soul.*"

In his opening essay to Pancake's book, McPherson tries to understand the ending of his student. He describes in Breece Pancake a compulsively giving young man, a person unable to ask for what he needs, spiritually. *How does one say he expects things from people after having cultivated the persona of the Provider?* McPherson writes. *How does one explain the contents of a secret room to people who, though physically close, still remain strangers? How does one reconcile a lifetime of indiscriminate giving with the need for a gesture as simple as a kind word, an instant of basic human understanding? And what if this need is so bathed in bitterness and disappointment that the attempt itself, at a very critical time, seems hopeless except through the written word?*

Young Andre and I talked about it. Andre said health—physical, mental—was more important than anything, eclipsed even writing, art. I agreed. We didn't say so at the time, but the McPherson piece seemed to speak directly to both of us. The sun was coming down in the trees, leveling, lighting an iron fence, a spit of snow across Kingsbury Avenue. Some wind at the glass rattled the windowpane a little, and the afternoon waned into dusk.

CHAPTER NINETEEN

All that spring I worried. About the future of my family; about my future at Bradford College. I needed just one more year to graduate—there were ways to do this, Andre assured me; I tried to be quiet about it, but I knew he felt my fear.

I didn't know, financially, how I would swing it. On a bright late April day, I sat with Andre and Dr. Patricia O'Malley, the Bradford Dean of Humanities, in her second-floor office of Coates House. Dr. O'Malley agreed to help me put together new grants and scholarships for my last year at Bradford, which would start the following fall. She was an energetic, caring sort with bright eyes behind glasses and cinnamon hair; her office was neat, academic, organized. Andre proposed and Dr. O'Malley accepted that I would do an independent study over the summer—I would write a story, and Andre and I would communicate through tape-recordings; this would earn a valuable six credits to help me round out the full credit count that I needed. Andre turned to me then, midway through all this discussion, humor in his eyes.

"And I'll need a teaching assistant next year. Know anybody who might want the job?"

•

A week later I was driving deep into Pennsylvania, on my way home to Illinois. Rolling hills, violet evening skies. It was a long, dusty trip and, late at night, on a bridge, the Chevette lost electrical power and steam started coming from the engine. The car just died; the bridge was long and narrow, over some sort of steep, shallow gorge, and I got out rather frantically and pushed the car down the slight incline until I'd cleared the overpass, then jumped in and swung the car onto the sandy shoulder, just as a large truck went barreling by, the heavy-air concussions close, rocking me. And then it was quiet, the sultry darkness all around. I didn't know much about cars. I'd been having troubles with my radiator and thought that if it was low and I filled it I might solve part of the problem—that maybe at least I could make it to a gas station then to wait for morning and mechanics. With a plastic bottle, I made my way down into the ravine, hoping for a stream in the darkness. There was one. I filled the bottle, scrambled again up the steep, wild grass face of the ravine, swearing at my luck. I filled the radiator, not caring about how filthy the water was. But the radiator was not the main trouble—I needed a new timing belt; I sat there under the stars, turning the ignition, hearing a stutter, sometimes just a click. Looked at my watch. It was almost three o'clock in the morning. More trucks went by, more air-concussions. Afterward, the sound of cicadas.

At some point, as night lightened into dawn, a cruiser pulled in behind me and a well-meaning policeman called a tow truck and got me to a nearby garage. At eight that morning the garage owner, an aging Marine, gave me a decent price on what the car needed—seals for the radiator, a new timing belt; thing was, the timing belt would come to them only in the afternoon. I was welcome to wait in the station.

I took Andre's new book, *The Times Are Never So Bad*—

it had just come out and he had signed this copy for me—from the passenger seat of the Chevette and stepped across the highway. I had a Snickers bar from the station vending machine and a bottle of water. A hill rose here in the morning, and in the new, humid air of the day I could see, at the top of the hill, a large, rather dilapidated hotel; before I reached it, I settled in the shade of a spreading oak tree and started into "The Pretty Girl," Andre's opening novella. The wind blew a little and cars came at a leisurely pace in and out of the hotel behind me, and sometimes I resented those people for having the money to stay in air-conditioned rooms: I could feel the day would be hot. Below me was the garage and, slightly off down the street, at an intersection, a McDonald's.

I fell into the story of Raymond Yarborough and Polly Comeau; the tale is initially narrated by Ray, Polly's former husband, a muscle-conscious, complicated man who has an insatiable need to continue possessing his former wife. He relies on terror to fill this need, to keep her close to him. One night in the past, we find out, he has broken into the home she is staying at and raped her by knifepoint. Now, as the story opens, he is contemplating more violence: he will beat a former lover of Polly's nearly to death; he will set a fire at the place she is staying now, all to announce that he remains in her life.

Haunting "The Pretty Girl" is the ghost of Ray's older brother, Kingsley, who has been killed in Vietnam; *"dead in the war we lost,"* Ray tells the reader. The story is about the Yarborough family's tragedy, and how Polly becomes the focus of Raymond's grief, tension, and rage. As in many of Andre's stories, the violence moves out from the center to find those on the periphery of the initial fury.

·

I was absorbed all morning in the reading. Occasionally I looked up when Amish carriages went by, drawn by horses. Sometimes the carriages turned into the McDonald's and stopped, the women and men dressed in their dark clothes descending, looking like they'd stepped from another century into all that commercialism. I read through the novella, then into the first short story, called "Bless Me, Father"; I put my mark in the book and slept and then walked to the McDonald's for an early lunch. I read "Bless Me, Father" and slept again under the tree, the heat disturbing my dreams, waking to a shimmering coming through the leaves. Then at about two o'clock, the Chevette was fixed and I thanked the Marine, showed him Andre's photograph on the back of the book, and told him Andre was a former Marine captain. The mechanic nodded agreeably.

He said, "Hope his book does well. Tell him *Semper Fi*. Drive safely, son." We shook hands, and the man filled the car with gas and I was on the road and I didn't stop again until I'd reached the far side of Indiana and was about to enter Illinois.

CHAPTER TWENTY

My parents' home was on a circle in St. Charles, forty-five miles west of Chicago. It was a small, low-slung modern structure set among heavy trees and sumac bushes. The yard fell to a slight ravine in the back, a gray and black pattern down there of shadows. The heat bore down on the plains, making the dry grass around the house brown. The sky outside the picture windows of the home was a steady blue, often cloudless.

Dad and Chris and I converted part of the garage into a workshop and built a small addition that extended the garage some sixteen feet to accommodate the length of racing shells. We installed our tools—a belt sander, a drill press, a long table covered in tough blue vinyl and outfitted with bench vices; we had a wall of hole-board and wire hangers to hold our hammers and hand drills and saws and chisels. We filled the drawers with sanding paper, bolts, nuts, and screws, the shelves with urethane and epoxy. We contracted out the basic hulls of the kayaks and the racing shells to a builder in Wisconsin, and periodically we drove there in Dad's silver Oldsmobile station wagon, equipped with a long roof rack, to pick the fiberglass hulls up. We finished off the boats in the new workshop. Though kayaking wasn't the popular sport it is today, we were known for our workmanship and that reputation allowed us to sell a steady stream of the Hurka *Expedition* and *Javelin* models. Because we'd had a number of incidents with the fiberglass craft getting crushed on trucks, especially with the long boats—the racing shells— we drove the long boats ourselves to fill individual orders in Wisconsin, Ohio, North Carolina, even once that summer to Princeton, New Jersey. It was a busy few months. Slowly, as Dad removed himself from the American Machinery job, we brought much of our extra equipment to a caged-off section of an industrial storage building in downtown St. Charles that Dad rented. To me, the giant warehouse was like a shadowed city of the stored dreams of American industrialists and entrepreneurs; the building was often, largely, in darkness, and when the lights were thrown on in a caged cubicle, they stretched wire fence and machine block patterns into the other units and across the huge cement floor.

•

I wrote every day in the early morning, even if we were on the road. I worked always in longhand in a record book. If we were home, in the evenings, I typed my manuscripts in an unfinished room in the lower part of the house; the old IBM Selectric sat on what used to be a kitchen counter.

One June weekend, while my family was visiting friends in Michigan, I had the house to myself, and I sat at the dining room table upstairs with my record book. Outside the sliding glass doors to the balcony, the sycamore and red sumacs were at the lush height of June, nearly July, and I described a harmonica player from the point of view of his brother, the lead guitar player in a Massachusetts blues band.

I thought at first I would somehow work the drummer into it and write about the murder, but the story took a different form. The culminating scene was based on a time Trice and I had seen River Street perform at a Knights of Columbus building in Lawrence, a year before, a series of bands playing, the floor jammed with people, a rumor floating around that one of the musicians on stage—the best saxophone player in the area—had been freebasing cocaine before the show. As I'd watched him I'd wondered: what would happen if he just collapsed—went into a coma in front of all these people? That question began to take over my work: that sax player became my harmonica player; I realized that my story was about the disintegration of young talent and the implosion of the band—of four men who depended on each other.

I worked on it and revised it and finally had a first draft, and I sent the story to Andre, and a few days later he sent me a tape-recorded response, a detailing of where I'd been too harsh with my first-person narration ("you're using the word 'fuck' too early," he told me. "You want to be careful with this; you need to establish the precise tone you are after. The choice you're making here will make your reader feel, initially, that your narrator is less sensitive than he is.") And Andre was concerned, as always, with the proportion of the story: some scenes needed to be expanded, he said, and some were repeating the same psychological information and needed to be cut. I went back to work on it, draft after draft. I followed Andre's instruction to tape-record myself reading final drafts to check that the music of the piece was right. By summer's end, I felt I'd created something a little more substantial than anything I'd done before. I called it "The Great White Bluesman." Eventually, it would help get me into graduate school—Andre was insisting, now, that I apply when the time came.

•

My room in the Illinois house was on the first floor, which was like a basement, set partially into the hill. It was cool down there, and shaded, and you could open a floor-to-ceiling, thin window so the summer air would move through. You could see the hill falling off and the tips of the scarlet sumacs. In the evenings, as the sky became violet, I read. Sometime in that early summer I made it to the final story in Andre's new collection, which begins *My name is Luke Ripley and here is what I call my life.* In Andre's "A Father's Story," Luke Ripley is fifty-four, a divorced Catholic, the owner of a horse stable. The stable has thirty horses and employs a group of instructors. At night, as shadows reach across his lawn, Luke listens to opera. He has four grown children, only one of whom he sees frequently now—his twenty-year-old daughter, Jennifer, who has come to visit him. Luke also has a long-time, close friend in Father Paul LeBoeuf, a local priest who has seen Luke through the lonely aftermath of his divorce.

Luke Ripley shares the suspicions of his author about the hierarchy of the Catholic church and the money that goes to the construction of places, rather than the poor. So, he doesn't give at Mass, at the time of collection; he sends his money to an organization in New York that feeds the destitute. "I know this is stubborn," he tells the reader, "but I can find no mention by Christ of maintaining buildings, much less erecting them of stone or brick, and decorating them with pieces of metal and mineral and elements that people still fight over like barbarians."

"A Father's Story" centers on one summer night when Luke has gone to sleep, and his daughter is out with friends. She comes home and wakes him, very late, to tell him that, after dropping off everyone, she has hit somebody on a lonely stretch of highway; she panicked, she tells her father, and drove from the scene of the accident. Luke drives his pickup to the place, praying not to find what he eventually does: a young man who dies just as Luke discovers him in the tall grass near the road.

Now Luke Ripley faces a moral choice—whether to leave the young man and hide the crime—or turn his daughter in to face the consequences of what she's done. He leaves the young man in the grass; he takes Jennifer's car and drives it in the early morning to Father Paul's church, where, pulling into the drive, Luke acts like he's fainted and smashes the car into a tree—giving an explanation for the damaged car and making his friend, Father Paul, who comes out to help him, an unwitting conspirator.

Luke knows that he must answer for all of this to God; in the end, the reader is given an intimate look at that conversation. Luke admits that he could have borne "with pride" watching his sons "take the whip and nails." *But,* he says to God, *You never had a daughter, and, if You had you could not have borne her passion.*

So, God says, *you love her more than you love Me.*

I love her more than I love truth, Luke says.

Very few stories can make me weep as I finish them. I still have that reaction at the end of "A Father's Story," no matter how many times I read it.

CHAPTER TWENTY-ONE

My job that fall was to sit beside my mentor in three sections of fiction writing and to keep detailed notes about the students. I did some tutoring as well. Andre took me into his confidence regarding student issues—sometimes, when he or I sensed that something wasn't right with a student, if there was a behavioral or performance problem, we went and looked into the student's background at the registrar's office.

I made copies of Andre's class materials, and often of his new stories—I remember working at the library copier, talking to Betty, the librarian, as the light of the machine ran in bright, steady rectangles, running off a novella that Andre had just finished. The novella was called *Voices from the Moon.* When Betty had gone to file some books, I looked down at the pages spilling precisely into the holding tray and wanted to become absorbed in them. Sometime soon after I did, borrowing an extra copy that Andre had me make—the compelling story of a fourteen-year-old boy who wants to be a priest, wrestling with the fact that his father and brother love the same woman. Soon there would be great interest from Hollywood in Andre's *Voices.*

It seemed to me that fall that suddenly the public began to know more about Andre Dubus. There were photographs being taken of him, interviews filmed with him. A photographer from *Time* magazine ducked into the classroom one day, just before class was beginning, to ask if he could possibly take a picture of Andre outside on the lawn. Andre laughed and told us he would be back in a moment—he had to go outside and be famous.

One evening as we were walking across campus, Andre recounted an interview he'd had that day—I can't remember what television program or documentary company it was for.

"They wanted me to do it in a hotel room they'd booked," Andre told me. "So we go in there with their television cameras and all their equipment: it must have looked like we were shooting a porn film. Soon after we started the woman doing the interview got fixed on asking me about 'A Father's Story.' There's that scene where I describe the pine trees rising over the church and she'd decided that meant that nature took precedence over religion, that organized religion was dying; she insisted on it. I tried to tell her I was just going for the image—that didn't make her wrong, but it wasn't my *intention* to say something symbolic in that moment."

He told me symbolism was a "secret weapon" that was sometimes used by writers, but not nearly as often as reviewers and academics would have you believe. Through my early attempts at fiction, I'd begun to understand by this point that a short story was usually about one, powerful thing, one explosion of thought, and was rarely constructed with the tiny, additional metaphoric excursions that some reviewers insisted were there. "A Father's Story" was about a father and a daughter, and a bond that transcended even the laws put forth by the father's God. Andre had tried to tell this interviewer in the hotel that, but she wanted the story to be about more, to be more embellished by the author's brilliance. He shook his head sadly at the memory now. "There was no convincing her," he told me.

CHAPTER TWENTY-TWO

Andre was writing at the height of his powers at this time, a period when his life, subtly, was beginning to fray. I think that some literary historians will probably draw a psychological connection between these; there will be some validity to this. But to me, watching first-hand, I sensed that Andre was just trying to survive his days. He was carrying his heavy teaching load, and disciplining himself to do his writing, and the interior-exterior see-saw that he had lived with for so long was beginning to pull him apart. His blood pressure was running high (he had been diagnosed with hypertension in 1981) and there were times, now, when I noticed that his eyes sometimes were frantic, and his face would quickly flush at the thought of some new responsibility, some new request. He was teaching five classes; he was lobbying the school to relieve him of one class in return for the advertising his writing brought the institution. Other professors had this arrangement—a reduction in classes for academic or professional projects—why couldn't he?

Andre had a peculiar blindness to him, a benevolence toward others (it was based in forgiveness, which nearly always won out in his spirit) and I felt he was not recognizing an animosity that was growing toward him with some in the administration. I was close enough to a number of faculty members by now that I'd heard the whispers, the things that were being said about him, and I thought events, day by day, were leading to trouble. There was a simple jealousy toward Andre, this popular, enormously talented writer and teacher—that jealousy took form in exposing how Andre violated norms. He was too close to his students, this thinking went; he formed friendships with them and went to bars with them. He was a Louisiana hick and fond of guns, kept a locker of them in his home (this, about the guns, was true). He dressed like some cowboy-biker-hippie. He was a little too wild for the academic world. One dean in particular seemed to be leading the charge, and she was convincing her peers. There were people, I began to realize, who wanted to see Andre gone from the campus altogether.

As these clouds gathered, he still gave his students excellent courses. For a contemporary literature class I was in, Andre brought in some of the writers we were reading. There was the young Susan Dodd: bright, vivacious, beautiful. Susan had just won the Iowa Short Fiction Award with her collection, *Old Wives' Tales,* and we were midway through her stories. She read to us from one of these and answered questions: she talked about how her stories were formed and how she'd studied at Boston University with Elie Wiesel, how she'd accompanied her mentor on one of his famous journeys to the Soviet Union in support of Andrei Sakharov, the nuclear physicist and dissident under house arrest.

These memories are strong and distinct; autumn sunlight through the windows of seminar D, where we had our literature classes as well as the workshops. Richard Yates stepping into the classroom one afternoon—he had been a teacher and dear friend of Andre's at the Iowa Writers' Workshop. I recognized him from his rather stern author portrait on the books of his I'd read, *Liars in Love* and *Eleven Kinds of Loneliness* and *Revolutionary Road:* in person, you saw much more of Yates' vulnerability. He was fifty-six years old and walked slightly stooped, his body once ravaged by tuberculosis. A highly intelligent face, bright eyes. He was gray-bearded and wore a jacket and casual shirt and slacks. He shared a quick, bawdy humor with Andre. Here was the creator of a story I'd been reading just the night before, called "Oh Joseph, I'm so Tired"—I'd found it a completely absorbing work, and now viewing the man himself, I saw the mischief and hope and despair that you found in many of his characters. Richard Yates was a modern Fitzgerald, a shrewd, lyrical witness to human behavior. Many years later, long after his death, I would see flashes of the writer I'd met in the actors who formed the ensemble of a television show he'd greatly influenced, called *Mad Men.*

Two times that semester Andre took us down the spiraling stairs, through the art gallery, and into the Bradford movie theater to see films he felt were important for us to view: an adaptation of Nadine Gordimer's "Town and Country Lovers," about the illicit affair between a white man and a black woman in the depths of Apartheid South Africa, and the terrifying Roman Polanski version of *Macbeth.* And we read, deeply, from the work of other writers whom Andre was close to and could tell us about: of Tobias Wolff, we read *In the Garden of the North American Martyrs.* Wolff had a powerful restraint in his work that had its birth, I thought, in Hemingway's prose—a bridled passion and a sly humor and an occasional, startling understatement. We went also through some of the twenty-five stories in Gina Berriault's collection, *The Infinite Passion of Expectation.* The volume—a paperback, a simple white book with elegant gray lettering—became a bible to me, and I read all of her stories over and again. I have a memory of being in my bedroom that fall on Cogswell Avenue, reading Gina Berriault, and outside the window, there was an old, towering blue spruce; the sun sparkling through its branches, the light lowering into evening, darkening brick walls of nearby houses, throwing shadows in triangles. Berriault's prose was wild, rich, and precise; I wanted to write like that. And her *perseverance* impressed me. In introducing her to us, Andre had told us her story: over a decade before, a major New York critic had torn apart Berriault's first, fine works of fiction—novellas called *The Son* and *A Conference of Victims.* The critic had said that reading Berriault's work was like trying to "read through peanut butter." He managed to do considerable damage to her career. Berriault soldiered on and finally came out with this new collection. Andre said that he knew Gina Berriault's work would one day take its place in the library of great American prose, and this has proven true.

CHAPTER TWENTY-THREE

Late that October, in Lebanon, a suicide bomber drove a truck with two thousand pounds of explosives into the barracks of U.S. Marine peacekeepers: two hundred and twenty Marines were killed, along with many other service personnel. It was the deadliest loss to the Marines since the battle of Iwo Jima in 1945.

Andre was in despair that day as we walked to the administrative building together to check on some student records—he was ranting in fury about the fact that the Marines had been *there* in the first place.

"Fucking Reagan should be on his *knees* in apology to those families," he said, waving his fist.

There was something about Andre's drama—I would have called it melodrama at the moment—that hit some button in me. I hadn't voted for Ronald Reagan, I told him, but I didn't think *any* American president should be on his knees in front of *anyone*.

We started to quarrel; I was worked up at what I thought of as a liberal, easy response that was not grounded in a practical understanding of the dark forces out there in the world. Andre was angry at what he saw as his more conservative protégé defending the powers that be. But within the hour

I was thinking very seriously about the emotions my friend had to be going through for his fellow Marines. And it *was* insane, the way the Marines had all been bottled up in one area, like the American forces at Pearl Harbor. As we were walking back to our first class, I said to Andre, "I'm sorry, man—I was reacting without thinking about how this must be for you. Of course, the goddamned administration fucked up." We calmed down about it and did our teaching for the rest of the day. We got mad at each other from time to time, but we never stayed mad for long.

•

There was a campus production of *Romeo and Juliet* slated for that semester, and Peggy Rambach had taken on the role of Juliet. During one early night of rehearsals, Andre called me at my apartment. He sounded sober but was not: Young Andre was living elsewhere now, and Cadence was off with a babysitter, he told me. It was a quiet night at home.

"Peggy at rehearsal?" I asked. I could hear Duke Ellington in the background.

"Oh no," Andre told me. "Peggy and I are just hanging out. She's right here with me."

I knew that wasn't right, and alarm bells went off in me. I walked, quickly, up toward the college—through the cool autumn evening, past the intersection with Route 97 and the old congregational church and apartment houses, through the college parking lot, by the library and over Tupelo bridge. At the dormitories, the evening shouts of college students and the sounds of their stereos gave a sense of normalcy to the falling light.

When I got to Andre's door, there was a note taped there, in Andre's distinctive handwriting, in French: *Dear friends and family—please enter, Peggy and I are upstairs listening to music!* Duke Ellington was blaring up there—what the devil was going on? The house here at the landing was in darkness, and I went through the door, up the steps that I knew so well now, to another landing and the kitchen, up two more steps to the right into the small den and sitting room. A low light was on, a cone of illumination that left everything else in distorted shadows. Andre had a set of drums in the corner that he couldn't really play very well, and that is where I found him, eyes closed, tapping with brushes to the rhythm of the music. Beside him, on the couch, there was an effigy he had carefully constructed from pillows. He had dressed the figure in Peggy's clothes, and put one of Peggy's hats on the head. He'd done a good job of it: I was startled, at first, thinking in that room of shadows that this was another person. Andre, when he realized I was there, was embarrassed, momentarily; he turned the music down so we could talk and I told him I was sorry to just come in this way, but the sign on the door said come in.

"Not to worry, pal," he said. "Great to have you."

"I just wanted to check on you," I said.

Peggy had been out constantly, he said, rehearsing her play: he was sick of it, this fucking play. I kidded with him about another man kissing his wife, and he laughed about the actor and the situation, *Fucking guy.* But I couldn't really get him out of his drunken brooding. I began to understand that the theatrics were for Peggy's return, to demonstrate his loneliness, his neglect. Andre had some great emptiness in him when he wasn't being attended to by women, a pattern

I would come to recognize after years of witnessing it: it was easy for him to feel abandoned.

I didn't want to be there when Peggy got home, but I didn't want my friend to be alone, and so I stayed with him, and we talked, and I think he was surprised that I had responded with such concern. When I heard Peggy come in the door I rose and greeted her briefly and then made my way out of there as she started to say to Andre, *What is all this?* I didn't want to stick around.

CHAPTER TWENTY-FOUR

It was November 1983. Andre's blood pressure had shot up to dangerous levels, and his doctor was telling him he was very much in need of rest. With or without a doctor's permission Andre was capable of a hypochondriacal crusade, and now he went full-on into trying to impress on others that that he needed to rest his beleaguered spirit. I think that often, because of his drama, people didn't entirely believe him, but I did. He had put everything he had into his writing and teaching for years, and he was psychologically and physically exhausted.

He called me one late afternoon and told me I would have to take over his fiction workshops for the week. One of those classes, with an older group of adults, was for that very night. A jolt of nervousness ran through me, an old self-consciousness that had haunted me, always, when I'd had to make speeches in high school.

"Andre, man, I don't know if I'm ready."

"You're ready. Just lead the discussion. Tell them about my health issues. It's a good group, they'll understand."

They did, thankfully. I started the class, feeling like a fraud—but the workshop was accepting, as Andre said they would be, and after the first reader had presented her work, the class plunged into discussion, same as always.

I was careful not to pretend, with any of the classes I took over for Andre during that time—it stretched to two weeks—that I had any knowledge superior to that of the students. I just led the discussions and was firm about that, and by the end of that time, I was enjoying the magic of teaching, of feeling at the center of the action. The nervousness, the fear of failure—these still visited me at the start of our classes, but they left quickly enough once we were underway.

For his substitute, Andre eventually brought in his agent, Philip Spitzer, who had an interest in teaching and wanted to explore this avenue as a possible career; Philip would fly in from New York and I would pick him up at Logan airport and we would drive back to the college and, especially for the older students, this was a great treat—having the perspective of a real live New York agent in class. Philip had a droll, riotous sense of humor, and we became good friends.

•

Meanwhile, I had applied to four graduate schools: the University of Alabama, the University of Arkansas, the University of Arizona, and the Writers' Workshop at the University of Iowa.

"Grad school is money in the bank," Andre told me one day as we were driving in his old Subaru, attending to chores in Haverhill. Some snow was coming down, feathering away from the windshield, Haverhill sliding by. "You'll have a two-year shelter to write in, and you'll put together a first book, and when you graduate, you'll have a teaching career ahead of you." He hand-wrote the recommendations he sent out to the universities, telling them that I was prolific, hard-working; he had faith that I would be published. He told each director openly that I would need money, a teaching stipend. I got into all four places, but it was Iowa I would go to, one state over from my family. In his quiet way, my father was happy when I told him on the phone. It was like he'd known, forever, that I would wind up a writer going to graduate school.

CHAPTER TWENTY-FIVE

I have often imagined a scene that followed, piecing it together as I heard it from others, and from Andre. Late one evening: Andre walking near the back of Academy Hall, slightly drunk, drifts of snow at the sides of the walkway. A large, loudmouthed student—I still don't know who the kid was—very drunk, proclaiming, "I want some *pussy,* man, show me the *pussy.*" Andre snapped that there were women around, this was a college campus, not a frat house, and then loud words between the two of them—the kid challenged Andre and they were grappling, swinging, the fight soon broken up by others who stepped in.

It was the excuse those against Andre needed: there was a steady push, then, to evict Andre and his family from campus housing. I made an appointment with a college administrator to protest; the administrator was a concerned academic who had helped me with my scholarships, a friendly, reserved man—I couldn't believe he'd go along with having Andre evicted from the campus after so much history here.

"I think this is way over the top," I said to him. "I mean, it was the student who was out of control."

"But Andre had been drinking, too," the administrator said, shaking his head. "And a college professor can't be getting physical with a student."

I see the administrator's logic now, of course, with time and distance, but then I was offended at this whole situation, a fierce warrior for my mentor. I said that Andre had put himself on the line for me many times, and that he'd done the same for many students. I emphasized how he'd helped me get into graduate school. "He's a serious educator," I said. "I don't see how one incident can get him evicted from his home."

The administrator said there were other incidents but would not elaborate. I still don't know what precisely he was referring to. But I slowly began to understand that the objections of a few, well-placed academics had made an impression on the administrator that he would not be turned from. I was out of my depth. "Andre's a good man," I said, in a last, rather desperate pitch. "I would trust him with everything I love. He's been the best professor I could have asked for."

"Duly noted," the administrator said.

Andre was a man of great pride, and the eviction meant, I knew, that he would leave Bradford College altogether. So my last year at the college would also be Andre's last; the end, as it turned out, of his formal teaching career. I could sense that he'd come to this reckoning in our walking and talking together. There was some bitterness, but not much, a sense of liberation, and some fear of what the future would hold financially. I knew a few of the people who had aligned against him, and though I brought them up in our conversations I was surprised that Andre didn't openly criticize them or fall into gossip, as I'm sure they did. He saved his opinions for his writing—in an open, final letter to Bradford president Arthur Levine, he outlined the health problems he'd encountered, the lack of help from the college, the demand that he keep teaching a full load, regardless. He spoke of all the students he was proud of, the fulfilling careers they'd gone on to. Then, as typical, he ended with a story: that on his first day of teaching at Bradford, he was nervous and one of his first students—a young woman—met him by happenstance in the snack bar and walked him to class and eased his tension. On his last day of teaching at Bradford another student walked him after his last class to the snack bar. *So what was it all for?* he asked President Levine. He hadn't worked on behalf of the cold, bureaucratic walls of the institution, he said—the college only afforded students and faculty a time and place to meet. No: not for Bradford; his efforts were *for that first student, and the last, and all the students in between.*

Andre did not come to graduation. It would have been a gesture of support for an institution that had treated him so shabbily—I drove around after the ceremony one last time to Andre and Peggy's campus housing, and there they greeted me and congratulated me and gave me, as a present, a beautiful collection of William Faulkner's work. *For good Joe and his good stories—* Andre had inscribed it, *Love, Andre. 15 May 1984.* The day was bright at the windows and despite everything that had happened to them Peggy and Andre seemed happy. Then it was time to go, and Andre said he would walk me back to the parking lot. The trees were swaying above us with wind.

"Andre," I said, "I don't know if I'll ever be able to thank you—" I broke down. He did, too. He gave me a bear hug and said, "I never say so long, man. I say I'll see you later. You do well at Iowa, buddy."

"I will," I said.

We turned away from each other quickly and I glanced back once, watching his figure walk back beneath the trees.

PART THREE

CHAPTER TWENTY-SIX

Iowa was acres of cornfields like golden seas, and relentless, quiet sun. At night, the moon was pale golden yellow over a violet, horizontal line.

I lived in an apartment I'd found on the Coralville strip, on 5th Street, in a busy area just outside Iowa City. My brother Chris helped me with the move in late August. I was the only tenant in a small, brick building that stood alone on the side of a parking lot, sunk a few inches into the ground. From my windows I could see three-story apartment buildings all around. There was wire fencing at the back of the lot with tangled, unorganized vines growing over it and, not too far beyond, a highway: I was located between the two thoroughfares, 5th Street and Route 6 heading west to Des Moines, east to Iowa City.

I had two simple rooms that were about evenly divided, each roughly sixteen-by-twelve feet. In the bedroom, we put my foam mattress (it was easy to travel with—it rolled right up) again on plywood and cinder blocks. There was fake, semi-gloss wood paneling on the walls. The place had the faint wood-smell of that paneling. I'd bought a tiny black-and-white TV that we set up on a plastic end-table by the bed; the TV always had a very precise picture. I put a cassette player and my guitars there, also, and I had two, fold-out aluminum beach chairs leaning beneath the bedroom window for when I might have visitors. The other room was made up of a small kitchenette, and in the corner, behind an orange, heavy-vinyl curtain, a toilet and a shower. There was a strangely raised section to the floor, facing the window here, where I set up my plastic garden chair and a rectangular card table and the Selectric typewriter. When the floods came, in the spring of the next year, I realized how useful the raised floor was for those things you absolutely needed to keep dry, like books and boxes of recording equipment and instruments and manuscripts.

I was a little over three hours from my family in Illinois. I drove the route back often, the long, straight shot of Route 80, helping Dad out where I could on many weekends and letting Chris know I was always close, which I thought was a help to him as he was going through his early teenaged years. I returned then across the cornfields; through Dixon, Illinois, over the Mississippi to Davenport, Iowa. In mid-October, the corn was harvested, the huge combines raising the dust of the earth. In winter, the land transformed into wind-blown snowy expanses. As I drove back and forth, I reviewed my schoolwork in my head—the workshop I was in met on Tuesdays, and our manuscripts were copied and left on a shelf of the university's English and Philosophy Building (EPB) a few days beforehand. So I carried these with me on my journeys and, driving, thought about what I would say to my classmates about their stories, the comments I'd written into the margins of their work; I was also in a literature class, and an advanced photography class. In one of the literature classes that year we read Andre's work, and I have a distinct memory of a grad student saying, with some awe, *Where's this guy been?*

Sometimes on my crossings that first autumn, the clouds rushed across the sky and the air turned a green color I had never experienced before: storms brewing, the possibility of tornados.

There were thirty thousand students at the University of Iowa then. They filled the downtown at night, a place which, with its cafes and bookstores, made you think of a small version of Cambridge, Massachusetts, set out on the wild plains. The dome of the Old Capitol building, the icon found printed on everything from scarves to notebooks to university stationary, was visible from various places in town, and you saw it lit and learned to judge where you were by your proximity to it. Writers with greater means than I settled in houses that radiated out from the center of Iowa City. I was making it on a little money that I had saved, and on a GSL—a Graduate Student Loan—and I had a stipend from the university for teaching one section of Rhetoric per semester to freshmen. I was determined not to take any money from my parents—they didn't have it to give now, in my opinion, much as I knew they would help in any way they could. Often, waiting in line at the Coralville grocery store a few blocks up from my apartment, I made quick calculations in my head, sweating out whether I had enough cash for my items. I lived close to the bone, but I had shelter, a place to write—everything I felt I really needed.

·

I couldn't afford phone service. When I wanted to call somebody, I went to a public phone booth at the corner of 5th and 1st Streets. The booth was plexiglass and blue, looking like it belonged in New York City rather than Iowa. It stood on a bleached, cracked sidewalk near some warehouses and I was under the impression that I was the only one who used it.

"I've got to admit," I told Andre, on one of my first September nights there, "I'm nervous about the teaching." I had my first Rhetoric class with the freshman coming up the next day.

"Well—" Andre said. He was speaking from the new house he and Peggy had purchased, on the outskirts of Haverhill. "You handled my classes fine when you had to take them alone. With these things, it's always like you're going into a large pool, and even though you think you're jumping into deep water you wind up realizing you're wading in the shallow end."

"I guess so," I said, doubtfully. "But I'm not just filling in here—I'm responsible for the whole thing."

"I know what you mean," Andre said. "I felt that way the first day I was teaching there, too. I walked in and it was hot in the building and I was nervous. I was trying to talk myself through it, but in the classroom all these faces were staring at me. I wanted to open a window, and then I had the thought: what if the window is stuck, somehow, and I can't get it open in front of these students?—I'm going to look like an ass. So I turned to all of them and I told them: *I want to open this but it won't look good if it gets stuck on me,* and they laughed with me, and I realized they were nervous, too. That was my first big lesson in teaching, to *speak your fear.*"

Andre calmed me down, though I was still worried when I took over my class on the first floor of EPB, all the students staring, just as Andre had described. That old high school terror of public speaking was moving in me, making my tongue tight (was it only vanity? Or something more serious—the fear that

I would fail Andre, fail myself, not be up for the job?). But I took Andre's advice and told them I was as nervous as they were on the first day, and soon we had broken the ice. I was always nervous about the upcoming classes, especially in the few minutes beforehand, but I also started looking forward to seeing these new student faces, experiencing the personalities as they became distinct to me. Over those first weeks, we all analyzed essays and wrote personal, critical, and argumentative papers that we workshopped (I usually did the assignments with them). The students were hardworking and intelligent, and we quickly became close. I took their papers home and typed responses to them that were far too detailed; my advisor, the renowned Rhetoric teacher, Cleo Martin, told me that my work ethic was admirable but that I was spending too much time on the papers.

"First of all," she told me, in one of our first conferences, "You've got to make things easier on yourself. Secondly, if you critique everything your students do, you'll overwhelm them. Better to concentrate in each paper on one or two things that they can improve."

On a steady basis, about once every two weeks, I met with Cleo; I would bring a number of my students' folders to Cleo's office in EPB—the Iowa River flowed right by her window there—and she would go over my students' work carefully with me, telling me how I might make my assignments more exact, how I might react better to student problems that came up. I thought of her, in time, as a trusted friend. So, I took it to heart when one day, after expressing satisfaction with the job I was doing, she looked at me and said, "Joe, I think you've found your calling."

•

My office was in the University of Iowa Library off West Washington. It was a cubicle in a small room of four that I shared on a revolving basis with other graduate students; I was usually alone in the hours I had scheduled there. In the hallway leading to the office, to your left as you entered the door, there was a giant, framed photograph of Abraham Lincoln looking at you: the Civil War was ending, the president's eyes infinitely tired, but with some satisfaction in them, too—some shred of grace after the nightmare he'd lived through. Many times, I stepped out to the hallway to look at those eyes.

It was in these first years that I began having a deep sensation with students that has never left me. In class, watching them bend to their work, thinking over something, writing, I realized the great love I had for them—an awe at human curiosity, at watching a young person figure a thing out, come to realizations. I told Andre about it, calling him one evening from the phone booth. It was growing colder and the sky over Route 6 was slate blue and orange.

"I know, man," he told me, about the students. "It's amazing."

At night, in what I called my bomb shelter of an apartment, I typed my manuscripts and student responses on the Selectric. I played guitar and recorded songs on a Fostex four-track analog recorder that had been a gift from my family for my Bradford graduation. I watched the news on the black-and-white TV—I think it only got two stations. Sometimes when I stepped out for a breath of autumn air, the moon was steady and high over the parking lot, and I heard the traffic on 5th Street and the turnpike, and saw the cars through the fence and ivy, all these vehicles rushing to their destinations in the Iowa night.

CHAPTER TWENTY-SEVEN

I was fortunate enough, in the lottery system through which we chose our workshop leaders, to get my first choice that semester. I couldn't believe I got to study with James Alan McPherson when, just a year before, Young Andre and I had been remarking over how much we thought of McPherson's introduction—his insight and wisdom—to the Breece DJ Pancake stories. In EPB, Jim shuffled into class with his trademark country gentlemen's cap, and he sat and looked around at his group carefully; ten of us looked back, all a little intimidated by his presence. Whatever dreams we had for ourselves, here was a man who had beaten greater odds than we could ever imagine to become an important voice in the country. I thought back over what I knew of him. He'd worked as a waiter on the Pullman Railroad, supported his family, put himself through school; he'd gotten an undergraduate degree in history from Morris Brown College in 1965 and gone on to study law at Harvard. He financed his first graduate degree by taking multiple jobs as a janitor, graduated in 1968, then earned an MFA at the Iowa Writers' Workshop in 1971. Much later in life, Jim and I would walk through Cambridge together, and he would show me the buildings he'd worked in as a custodian. He told me that when he was not working or studying law or writing his stories, he was in the Harvard library with earphones on, listening to Shakespeare plays on record.

At Harvard, studying with Professor Alan Lebowitz, Jim had produced his first short stories. One of these, called "Gold Coast," was subsequently published in *Atlantic Monthly*, giving Jim a national platform. Other publications in *Atlantic Monthly* followed, including groundbreaking nonfiction; an article of his in 1972 homed in on exploitive business practices against black homeowners. Collections of Jim's fiction were published by the Atlantic Monthly Press: the acclaimed *Hue and Cry*, in 1969, and *Elbow Room*, which won the Pulitzer Prize in 1978—Jim was the first African-American to win the Pulitzer. He was working at the University of Virginia then, and he didn't actively advertise the award: he was going through a divorce that year and sensed that, in the southern court system, the recognition would work against him.

As I sat before the man himself now, for the first time, I remembered my introduction to his work in Russell Banks' literature class in New Hampshire; Jim's early story (and one of his finest) called "A Solo Song: For Doc." "Doc" is a tale about an aging Pullman waiter whose company is trying to drive him into retirement—a man, proud of his work, up against the White machine. A fellow waiter narrates the story: I remembered the sensitivity and precision of the writing, a metaphoric portrait of racism so compelling that I felt what Doc felt—how age and circumstance and raw prejudice threaten to rob the man of his vocation and dignity.

•

Jim was quiet, shy, accessible to his students, unfailingly kind. He thought what you said through carefully, his eyes looking down as he considered, then back up to yours as if to touch base, to reassure you that he was still concentrating on the subject at hand. He frequently displayed the wry humor his stories demonstrated, and had a delightful, unbridled chuckle. Deep within him, despite all he'd witnessed during formative years in the Jim Crow south, was an unconditional love of humanity. In *Elbow Room* he wrote, *"I think that love must be the ability to suspend one's intelligence for the sake of something. At the basis of love therefore must live imagination."*

Jim expected you to be immersed in your work and was always encouraging you in his quiet way. He would begin class usually with some philosophical thought—about something that had just been in the news, or a book he had been reading. He had private conferences with us the day after our workshops. One expression we heard a lot in these meetings was, *that's a book you should get under your belt.* He was often gently pointing out a dimension you had ignored in your most recent work—for me, in my first conferences with him, he wanted my prose more grounded in the atmosphere and geography of setting, what he called "the blood of the place—it's like a character in and of itself." I concentrated on it until I felt, from his reactions, that I was succeeding. "*All* right," he said, quietly—his habit, a way of letting you know he was satisfied with the communication that had happened. "*All* right."

I expressed, in one of these early meetings, my admiration for Breece Pancake's work; Jim cast his eyes down on his desk a moment and nodded, confirming his own admiration for his former student. Then he looked at me with his large eyes. "Now, you take care of *your*self," he said.

•

In one of our first workshops we were minus a class member, a somber, red-bearded fellow who usually sat by the windows. The story was that this student had found the Iowa workshop atmosphere too competitive and had left the program. We whispered among ourselves, waiting for Jim to come in. I wondered how he would address the situation. Some said they felt the student had suffered from a great loneliness. I looked at the chair where the student usually sat—we had left it open in case he came back—and thought that I should have recognized this, what the writer was going through: goodness knows, I'd been lonely myself in my first days here. Then Jim arrived. He sat at the desk and gazed at us a moment. He looked at the empty chair and back at us. He said, *I want you all to understand that you're not competing with each other; you're competing with history.*

James Alan McPherson was then and to his last days the conscience of the Iowa Writers' Workshop. His thoughtfulness and intelligence seemed to be all around you: you felt it at faculty-student gatherings, both academic and social. When you first met Jim his quiet nature could be frightening, because you knew what a genius he was and reasoned he was judging you. But that wasn't the case: Jim was initially wary of most situations—that's what the quiet was about—but soon his measurement was because, once he thought of you as a benevolent spirit, he was looking for ways to benefit your ambitions and life. He was famously far-sighted in his vision of where the lives of his students would go, where our capabilities were.

It didn't take long for us to bond with Jim, relationships that lasted a lifetime.

•

At the phone booth one cool October night I told Andre about Jim, and Andre said, *That's a great guy to work with; he sounds like an interesting man,* and I said that Susan Dodd had come to visit me—we'd had lunch together—she was due soon to join the Iowa faculty herself. This news about Susan made me especially feel that I was gathering a family around me, as she was close to Andre and it felt like a part of him would be at Iowa soon, too.

I told Andre, and Susan, and Jim—and nobody else—that in addition to the short stories I was writing, I was beginning to experiment with stories my father had told me on our rides across the country to deliver boats, about his work and the work of friends of his in the Czech Resistance during the war, and his efforts in the Underground against the Czech communist government afterward. We'd filled many hours with these recollections. My writings were, thus far, sketches of both fiction and nonfiction—I was collecting them in a kind of scrapbook without having any idea of what I would do with them—maybe I would fictionalize them all, eventually, for my workshop sessions? Maybe I could simply produce a collection of true stories about human resistance? I didn't know. The stories seemed to reach deep into me, to somehow speak to my fear of family trauma and separation.

"You just keep writing," Andre said to me, one night in the phone booth. "The work will tell you what direction to go in. See where it all takes you."

In my bomb shelter in those Iowa nights, I fell into history: I wrote about operation *Anthropoid;* a family friend who lived here in the United States—the leader of the largest Resistance group in Czechoslovakia during World War II—had been involved in the planning of this operation. Because he was something of a prized uncle to me, and my father had told me his history, I'd read a number of accounts of *Anthropoid* as a boy. *Anthropoid,* conceived by the exiled Czech president, Edvard Benes, and Winston Churchill, set out to assassinate the Nazi leader Reinhardt Heydrich, architect of the Final Solution and the cruel Nazi head of Bohemia. The ultimate goal of the operation, beyond eliminating Obergruppenfuehrer Heydrich, was to send fear through the Nazi hierarchy that all Nazi leaders were in imminent danger. In May of 1942, two Resistance fighters intercepted Heydrich's Mercedes as he came into Prague one morning; one of them threw a heavy bomb at the car, and Heybrich succumbed to his wounds within days. The Resistance fighters took refuge in the Church of St. Cyril and St. Methodius on Resselova Street, joining five other members of the Czech-army-in-exile; the Czech patriots eventually endured a seven-hour standoff with four hundred SS troops and finally took their own lives.

In reprisal for the assassination, Adolf Hitler destroyed two Czech towns, Lidice and Lezaky, razing them to the ground (this was not far from my grandparents' home in Radnice), and brought a sustained horror down onto the Czech nation—thousands were executed; many political prisoners perished, including the priests and officials of the church, who were shot by firing squads that September.

The Nazis came for a search of my grandparents' home. My family was fortunate that these were regular, Wehrmacht troops and not SS. The soldiers were required to spend a half-hour in each residence. They spent the time playing a mandolin that my grandparents kept on the wall, singing songs. I've always felt that the mandolin, which I still have, was an angel of mercy for my family.

•

My first attempt at writing about *Anthropoid* was from the point of view of one of the Resistance men; I had spent a good deal of time with our family friend, the Resistance leader, playing chess with him when I was a teenager, and I borrowed his personality—bold and highly intelligent and self-deprecating—for the personality of my fictional freedom fighter. But as I wrote I realized there was still much I needed to know about the history of Czechoslovakia—there were great gaps in my knowledge of the time, especially in writing close to the consciousness of a native. Jim's concern with geography came into play here, as well: I needed to know more about Bohemia—what did Prague look like, on a very early morning in June? What did the metropolis around the church look like? What was the atmosphere of a small Bohemian town that my Resistance fighter would have lived in as a boy, that he would be remembering now, as the SS gathered around the church in what he recognized as his last moments? Jim would coach me to get a better handle on the geography, that this would lead to greater solidity and veracity with the character. I needed to see the Czech lands—not an easy thing for me, as my father's enemies were still in power there—or experience them somehow, and my writing was still uncertain work, the beginning of a long journey.

CHAPTER TWENTY-EIGHT

I went to every event in Iowa City—literary and musical—I could make it to; I was at readings of Andre's friend Tobias Wolff, and the poet, John Ashbury. Bob Shacochis' reading of his acclaimed short-story collection, *Easy in the Islands,* was like a small rock concert. In the spring of my first year, Russell Banks was touring with his new novel, *Continental Drift,* and I volunteered to ferry him around town in the Chevette. I was embarrassed about a repair I'd had to do on the passenger side of the car: there was a hole clear through the floor, and I'd fixed the problem with a metal road sign I'd found that fit nicely over the area. I'd covered it all with a rug, but my efforts still looked pretty pathetic. I told Russell about it and he looked down and laughed and told me what a classy man I was.

"At least the rain won't come up through—will it?" he said, a little doubtfully, looking more closely at my handiwork. We talked about New England College, and about what I'd done since. When he learned I'd studied with Andre Dubus, Russell said, "Of all the writers working now, he's the one we will remember."

I spent a great deal of time with Susan Dodd—Susan would soon write a masterpiece called *Mamaw,* a novel about the psychological journey a mother takes, grappling with the dark natures of her sons—Frank and Jesse James.

I have these fragments of recollection: a party in my second autumn in Iowa, outdoors on a lawn of Iowa City; lovely Susan in a blue dress coming across the grass, tossing her head back and laughing at something said by a student; the young writers sitting cross-legged with paper plates of bratwurst and hamburgers and potato salad. The leaves of a willow tree drifting over the grass before the cracked tar road—I'm not sure where we were, in front of a house someone was renting, perhaps Susan.

I saw huge concerts with friends at the new Carver-Hawkeye arena: Stevie Nicks, Alabama, Crosby, Stills and Nash. At the Crow's Nest one night in downtown Iowa City, Junior Wells and Buddy Guy performed together, bright figures in spotlights on the distant stage; I watched them over an enthralled sea of an audience. Their blues, so crisp and powerful, felt supernatural in that remote Iowa setting.

I went to many concerts alone: Ray Charles and Bonnie Raitt and John Prine and BB King. I watched BB King from the balcony of an elaborate theater on the Iowa River, across the water from EPB. King had a habit of slapping the back of his fist against the palm of his other hand in rhythm with the music. When he played "The Thrill Is Gone," I closed my eyes and listened carefully, and when I opened them, he was standing below me, his eyes closed, his face back and glittering with sweat, hitting the high lead notes on his guitar, Lucille.

•

It was later into my stay in Iowa now, my second year. There was a lover: a grad student, a teacher of French. She lived in the heart of Iowa City, and I drove in the cold autumn night, people bundled and moving stiffly down sidewalks. Shops and offices were mostly dark then; above me, chimneys were black shapes against the sky. I parked and went around to the side of the apartment building, up wooden steps, let myself into her apartment without turning on the light. Our relationship was physical, friendly, daring. Deep down, I'm not sure why, we both seemed to laugh at the suggestion of anything more involved. Her apartment was remarkably warm on that cold Iowa night; shadows, heavy lace cloth draped on the windows, the quiet tick of the radiators. A Rodin poster, a sculpture of a torso, was over her desk in the living room. Her notebooks were stacked there; my lover's sweater rested on the back of the desk chair. I made my way through the dark kitchen into the bedroom. She liked for me to arrive in the night without notice, to undress and slip into bed with her and wake her. The moon came through the curtains; her blonde hair was almost white on the pillow. She turned to me. Her eyes opened, sleepy, then bright with welcome.

•

In the Iowa Workshop our revolving mentors each had their own strengths, and brought us significant insight into why our stories were or were not effective. I worked first with Jim, then Robley Wilson, the rigorous editor of the *North American Review,* then Susan Dodd, and finally in my last semester, Jim again. We student writers had our successes and failures; many of our stories were too experimental, but usually these efforts were applauded for what they chanced. In one of the workshop groups there was a woman who, I felt, was particularly critical of my work (she was so with everybody's work, I realized with time and distance—but she had a unique ability in making you think you alone were her target). She was highly articulate and unsparing in her opinions. In the classroom, I always acted like her criticism didn't hurt me, then drove home swearing.

"Honest to God, Andre," I said in the phone booth. "The woman was wearing raptor's claws for earrings at the last Workshop party. I'm not making this up. She'll just scare the piss out of you. She's small but fills up the *room* with her fucking judgment. My last workshop she started things off by saying 'let's look at the grammar in this piece,' and she went on and ripped me to shreds."

Andre, despite himself, howled with laughter. "Did you fuck with the grammar?"

"I was trying to work with a lot of sentence fragments," I said, defensively. "It was sort of a botched deal, but there was still some merit to the story."

"I'm sure there was," Andre said, trying to take me seriously. He was struggling—the image of me under siege by a tiny woman with raptor's claws for earrings, I could tell, was hilarious to him. "*Raptor's claws—*" he said. "*Holy shit.*"

"I can't even write now," I said, miserably. "I sit down to get some words and there she is on my shoulder saying, '*Let's look at the grammar in this piece.*'"

"Well, fuck it," Andre said. "Put me on the other shoulder. Let us go to war."

"I'll try it," I said. "I'll try anything at this point."

"How long have you been having trouble with the writing?"

"It's been about three weeks now."

"Jesus, buddy. She really got under your skin. 'Course you better get used to it. You'll face worse than that from critics at some point."

"I know that's true," I said.

Andre paused a moment, thinking. "When I was out there," he said, "I wrote a novel that I realized, finally, just didn't work. I decided to hold a funeral for it."

"A *funeral?*"

"I wrapped it in some black crepe paper and we walked the book out to this backyard gravesite I'd dug. I'd invited my friends and neighbors and we had Beethoven playing on the record player. Kurt Vonnegut lived across the yard and came over and watched as we lowered the novel into the hole and he said, '*Andre, that's the saddest fucking thing I've ever seen.*'"

On my way back from the phone booth I kept breaking out in a grin—at Kurt Vonnegut staring into the hole and making his pronouncement, and at my own defensive stupidity. Who cared if someone didn't like my story, anyway? Others had seen some value in it and the truth was, when you got down to it Raptor's Claws was kind of right, the story didn't really hold together. It was an attempt, a steppingstone.

It was freezing and I jammed my hands into my pockets. The moon was high and pale over the telephone wires. Later, in the warmth of my apartment, I sat at the card table and wrote, mostly without the ghost of my critic. I was in Bohemia: I was describing the atmosphere of a small Czechoslovakian town in the 1930s. I had some photographs to go by, and I was reading about Czech history, and my father had recently told me in a phone call that the environment of central Bohemia, where he was raised, was similar to what you would find in New Hampshire. That gave me a sense of the wind there, the wild grass, the greenery. I imagined the stone walls and tight houses, my fictional young Resistance fighter walking the streets of his home. When my critic stole into my thinking,

I thought of what Andre said: "*Put me on the other shoulder.*" I remembered the winter evenings of walking with Andre at Bradford College: his profile in shadows, his face emerging in the campus lights we went beneath.

"I'm beginning to understand this," I'd told him one night: this came back to me. "You write about an individual, but you're representing all of humanity in your character."

"That's it," Andre had said, turning to me. "That's the whole fucking thing."

CHAPTER TWENTY-NINE

November 1985. Susan Dodd's former professor at Boston University, Elie Wiesel, was coming to speak at the University of Iowa; Susan was due to introduce him. Wiesel had just won the Nobel Peace Prize; he was also frequently mentioned in the news because, in April, in a ceremony at the White House where he was being awarded the Medal of Freedom, he had objected publicly to Ronald Reagan's impending visit to Germany's Bitburg cemetery where Waffen SS troops were buried ("that place, Mr. President, is not your place.")

On the night of the lecture, I made my way into the huge university auditorium, immaculate blue carpet underfoot, chandeliers already dimming. There was a big crowd seated, milling about, talking; many were in the aisles, settling against the walls if they couldn't find a seat. I had the sense of a great many Europeans in the audience. I found a space on the wall, close to the front. When Susan and Elie stepped quietly out from the stage door, the applause was immediate and thunderous and went on for a long time.

The author told us of his time with President Reagan, and said that, while he was grateful for the honor bestowed on him, he didn't feel he had much chance of getting a job at the White House as a planner of itineraries. He spoke then of his love of Kafka, of Kafka's brilliance and modesty. Watching Elie Wiesel, my thoughts drifted: images came to me of the life of strength and horror and endurance and faith he had lived, and I was struck by the intelligent, composed presence of the man. As a boy he had survived Auschwitz; had seen his family destroyed in the Holocaust—the word he himself had come up with for the Nazi genocide; Wiesel's subsequent memoir *Night* had been published to almost no notice initially, in 1960, but now had been translated into thirty languages and was one of the most widely-read memoirs in publishing history.

Though I knew the details of the author's story, I'd been trying to read *Night* for the first time that week; I'd wanted to have it finished by the time of this lecture. But I'd kept stopping, turning away from the book, emotional. I'd long known I would have this problem: I'd put off reading the book for years. I couldn't get through it, this harrowing, honest writing, this suffering at the hands of totalitarian intimidation and violence. Elie's prophet in the book—Madame Schachter—was ominous at the start of the piece; a middle-aged woman with her ten-year-old son on the packed cattle car to Auschwitz, insane already with the separation from the rest of her family. Having visions, seeing flames, wailing in fear so much that some of the other prisoners went from tolerance to violence with her, beating her, tying her up, gagging her. Fourteen-year-old Elie arriving with all of them at night, crowded together, their train stopping at this mysterious new place—Birkenau—the young author looking out the train at flames "*gushing out of a tall chimney into the black sky.*"

History was standing before me. Here Elie Wiesel was, the grown man—he had truly gone through all that; he was speaking now of rediscovering faith after great trauma. He finished with a story: about an old man who carries signs throughout his city, speaking out against injustice. A boy joins him in carrying the signs, and the two of them are a team for a number of years. Then the boy goes off to college and when he returns he asks the old man what has been changed by all the ranting, all this parading with signs. *Since you're young, I owe you an answer,* the old man says. *I used to carry the signs to change the world. Now I carry them so that it doesn't change me.*

•

Directly after, in a hallway behind the auditorium, Susan leaned out a door and beckoned for me to come into a small waiting room.

My first impression, close up, was of the author's eyes—eyes that had seen too much, but that still, somehow, found moments of humor and hope. I nervously greeted Elie and told him how much I admired him and what an honor it was. He and Susan quickly put me at ease. Susan said my family was from Czechoslovakia and Elie spoke again of Kafka. Then he asked what I was working on, and I plunged into telling him that I was writing about the Heydrich assassination, that my work was based partly on a family friend who had been involved in the planning of *Anthropoid.*

"That was quite a resistance," Elie said. His eyes moved into sadness. "So your family friend was murdered?"

"No," I told him. "He stayed in hiding during that time and went on to fight against the communists and then came to the United States. He lives in Wisconsin now."

I could see that the author was surprised by this—of course he would assume that anyone involved in the assassination would have been found and killed, with all the violence that Hitler brought down on Czechoslovakia in the aftermath. But Elie and Susan were overdue for their next engagement, and we didn't have time to further the conversation. I thanked them and went back out to the auditorium—it was still crowded with people, talking, shaking hands, hugging, discussing. I walked back to my car, swallowing down my emotions, thinking about the brave man I'd met, his firm handshake, his deep eyes. It was raining and the lights of cars shone in the black tar. I went through the parking lot, hunched in the rain. Cars hissed by me, finding the exit, indistinct faces behind water-beaded glass. Many of the cars held families that had come out to see the great man. I thought about how families from all over the world fell into the mad dreams of dictators—became prisoners suffering, often lost one another forever. In the heart of Elie Wiesel's work was the simple wisdom of witness and vigilance—a constant effort to keep history from being erased, to remind humanity to resist the will of totalitarian regimes. The Nobel Prize Committee had called him a "*messenger from God. His commitment originated in the sufferings of the Jewish people but expanded to embrace all oppressed people.*"

I found the Chevette and started it up and drove home, full of thought, in the autumn rain.

CHAPTER THIRTY

It was summer now in Iowa. Late July. The corn grew tall and made angled shadows on the ground, and the skies were dusty, red in the evenings, from the farmers' machines. I was packing up my things in Coralville to leave when a letter arrived. It was from Enid Thuermer, the mother of my childhood friend, David, in Boxford. Enid had sent a clipping from *The Boston Globe*, and a note. *Joe—I wasn't sure if you'd heard about this. –ET.* In the clipping there was a picture of Andre, an author's photograph I recognized from one of his books. There had been an accident on Route 93 North, at night, outside Boston. The article said that Andre Dubus had been trying to help stranded motorists and had been hit by a car. He was in critical condition at Massachusetts General Hospital.

It had been several weeks since I'd spoken to him. I'd called in May to thank him again for my grad school experience, to tell him none of it could have happened without him. I could hear his voice now in my head as I looked at his picture; he'd congratulated me. He'd happily told me that he and Peggy were expecting again. The summer was beautiful in New England, he said. He was getting ready to watch the Red Sox that evening, so life was good.

"*Congratulations again, compadre,*" he told me. "*Thanks for calling. Love you, man.*" His voice was as clear in my head now as if we'd just talked moments ago.

·

The accident happened late on the night of July 23, the *Globe* said. That was many days past. I hadn't heard anything about it: his family and friends, understandably so involved in the immediate trauma, hadn't told me. I made phone calls now to Young Andre, to Jeb and Peggy. I got the soonest flight I could and sat in the plane, anxious, reviewing all I'd been told as the aircraft whistled through the atmosphere. Andre had been driving home, coming back from doing research in Boston for a screenplay he was writing. Far ahead of him a drunken motorcyclist skidded out in the third lane of the four-lane highway and walked away, leaving his battered bike where it had fallen. Another car came on and hit the motorcycle—inside this car were a Puerto-Rican brother and sister, Luis and Luz Santiago; I imagined them coming to a terrible, ragged stop, getting out, cars and trucks whizzing by. In the heat and emotion of the moment, they convinced themselves that the motorcyclist must be lying on or by the highway—that perhaps they'd hit him, too. They were out and looking everywhere for him—at the side of the road, under their car, when Andre, seeing the commotion ahead, put on warning lights, slowed, pulled over to help. There was another car in the breakdown lane, two women already calling the state police on an emergency call box. Andre got out and was leading the Puerto-Rican sister, Luz, off the highway, when a driver in a Honda Prelude—confused by the lights and parked cars—veered to avoid the scene and went directly toward Andre, Luz, and Luis. Andre had just enough time to push Luz to safety, and then he and Luis Santiago were struck. Luis Santiago was killed; Andre, his legs shattered by the impact, was thrown up and over the Prelude, ending up on the trunk. Much later, when I asked him about it, he said he remembered only the lights coming at him.

Andre had thirty-four broken bones. In his first night at Mass General, his lungs started filling with marrow and the doctors didn't think he would make it to morning. By daybreak, somehow, the marrow had cleared—the doctors spoke of it as something of a miracle—but soon they were discussing amputating Andre's left leg. That was the current state of things. When I'd spoken with her Peggy told me that, just the night before, one of Andre's arteries had burst, and he'd nearly died again.

"It's very serious," Peggy said.

•

The first time I saw Andre after the accident he was heavily sedated with morphine. All but his face was covered completely in white sheets, and there was a kind of tent contraption where his legs were. We were in a glassed-off trauma section of Massachusetts General and he looked, with his beard, like some old-world figure laying there, close to mortality: it took the breath out of me. My sense, as I think about this moment, is that I was with Young Andre and Jeb, the sounds of hospital machinery surrounding us, the sounds of Andre—all of us—breathing.

I stood in the room and watched Andre carefully, his gray face. At least his breathing was steady. There was a light on above him, but his eyelids did not flutter. Somebody—a nurse—switched the light off and Andre's face was in shadow then. It seems to me that I stepped out of the room with Jeb and Young Andre and they were explaining what the doctors were saying, that the amputation was looking more certain. Looking back on this, on these first images of Andre at the start of his great trial, I realize now, writing these words, that I was in some state of shock. At some point that day Andre woke and I leaned down and hugged him, carefully, his eyes drugged but glad; he smiled, *Hey good to see you, buddy, thanks for coming.* Soon after, his orthopedic surgeon was there and opening the bandage over the gravely wounded left leg. I saw it. There didn't seem to be much of a leg left: from the knee to the ankle was open, just a pool of blood and flesh and muscle. A series of silver rods went down into that pool, apparently holding Andre's bones together.

"Are you sure you have to amputate?" I asked the orthopedist, quietly, later; the doctor, Young Andre, and I were on a long hallway walk together. It was late afternoon now, and below the hallway windows cars were whizzing steadily over Storrow Drive. The Charles River glittered in the last sunlight.

The doctor shook his head in sorrow. "We've been on the fence about it. But now the danger of infection is just too great." The doctor's young, intelligent face seemed full of contained emotion—he had evidently grown close to Andre and the family quickly. "I'm afraid that's the safest course now."

I took the train that night from North Station toward the North Shore, to the Haverhill stop. The weather was unusually cool, and I was glad for the warmth of the train-car. In my haste to fly, I hadn't watched the weather reports and hadn't brought a heavier jacket—I had only a windbreaker.

I'd told Andre this in our brief conversation: he said to go to his house in Haverhill in the morning and pick out one of his jackets. I would drive there before coming to the hospital tomorrow. The train smashed through the evening, the flickering lights and building-shapes of Ballardvale, Andover, Lawrence, Bradford—these names of the North Shore that signified home to me—the rushing dark leaves of trees and scalloping of telephone lines. I brooded into that darkness, hating what was happening to Andre, wishing I could take the pain from him, knowing there was nothing, pragmatically, I could do beyond showing up and providing a boost, some resilience, maybe ask him what errands he wanted me to tend to as long as I was here. I would stay with him, I determined now, through the amputation, if that was what was to come.

•

I was renting a Dodge Dart from Enterprise. I was staying with Enid Thuermer in the modular-cedar home that I had stayed in so many times in my life when her son David and I were kids. The window of the room I was in looked out on a yard of crushed bark, the forest just beyond. In these first cool nights in the woods of my old town, I dreamed of Andre and his accident, and woke to nightmares of his dismemberment; one night it wasn't Andre I dreamed about but my father, being carried, alive and bewildered, in a coffin to his own burial. I woke in a sweat, looking out the windows at the silent oaks and elms.

Each day I drove the Dart to the parking lot of the commuter train in Haverhill, sometimes going in alone, sometimes meeting up with Jack Herlihy, another close friend and former student of Andre's, sometimes riding with Young

Andre or Jeb or Suzanne. When we reached him, Andre was more awake now, often, more animated, always glad to see us. His single room was high at a corner of the building, the light in the afternoons stretching through the space. Some days, when I went in alone, I took notes for him as he kept up work on an anthology of American short stories he was editing, called *Into the Silence.* It helped, I think, offer him some sense of routine, of life continuing. At one point he suggested we include a new story that I'd just written. I looked up, surprised and humbled.

"That's generous of you, buddy, thank you."

"Generous—hell, boy, you earned it. You wrote a good story."

Frequently there were gatherings of people in that room when you got there: old friends, former students. Andre was cheerful with his visitors, honest about the situation he was in, and the contact with others seemed to infuse him with energy. "When you think about it, I'm lucky," he told a group of us one day. "There's a guy down the hall in his twenties going through the same thing. Poor man. I had my legs for fifty years."

Outside Andre's room late one morning as I came in a woman, a former student, had just finished visiting and was shaking her head with tears in her eyes. I asked her if she was all right.

"I came here to cheer *him* up," she told me, wiping her cheek, "and he winds up raising all of *our* spirits."

•

The night before the amputation, some two weeks after I'd flown in, I had a few minutes alone with Andre. He told me that he was getting through all of this by concentrating on God, his family, and the Marines.

"You're a brave soul, Andre," I told him.

He shrugged a little. He was resigned to this, facing it. "I don't know what else I can do," he told me. "You've just got to get through it. You've got to keep going."

I left the hospital late that evening, somber, walking toward North Station. Andre had been swapping jokes with me when I left but he didn't deny he was nervous. It was still very cool and I zipped up his tan leather jacket and there was the feeling, in the metropolis, of being under stage lights and then, in the next moment, of stepping through shards of darkness, anonymity. I thought, grimly, of my friend's mortality: I hoped the operation would go all right, that Andre could take it after all he'd been through—eleven procedures thus far. It was well past rush hour and cars drove by me quickly; steam came from gratings. The T rolled over iron bridge here, the sudden, heavy rushing shadows flickering over the broken-tar pavement. Across the street from me there was a pornographic theatre, a lone business open in an otherwise abandoned brick building that went the full block. Garish ads of porn stars were tacked up around the entrance on green-painted plywood, women with eyes of invitation and full, pouting lips. You could tell which men were headed there by the purposeful way they walked in the shadows, a squaring of the shoulders and tightening of the body that spoke of their wish to be completely unnoticed, to vanish into their yearning. They turned into the glass, black-papered doors.

·

I went to MGH early on the day after the operation. I was due to fly from Logan that afternoon. Andre and I were alone in the room for a few moments. He was pale, relief on his features, heavily drugged with morphine again. That knee area—they'd amputated just above it—was in pain, he told me. *It's not too bad,* he said. We talked about phantom pain, how strange it was, what the body and spirit were capable of. I tried not to glance at the empty angle of depression under the white hospital blanket.

"I put the coat back in your closet," I said.

"Thank you, man."

"Thank *you*—It would have been an uncomfortable stay without it. While you've been creating drama in here, it's been a challenge for those of us who have to walk around in the cold, real world."

"I guess I *have* been preoccupied," he said, smiling.

He was glad the danger of infection, at least from the open wound, was over. "*Man,* I can't wait to get home," Andre said, leaning back into his pillow. "Back to some kind of normal life."

A doctor came in. I realized they had things to talk about and said my goodbyes, leaning heavily on humor to get out of there without becoming emotional. *I'll see you, pal,* I said. I told Andre to behave himself with the nurses and the doctor smiled, and Andre and I saluted one another. Then, out of his sight, I leaned against the wall outside his room, not willing to go quite yet.

I heard Andre's voice say, "That fucking leg around the knee is killing me—"

This was a younger doctor, a resident I hadn't met before. He said, "Often people feel the sensation in the farthest part from the body, in the foot that isn't there anymore—"

"How long does it last?"

"There's no telling. It's a different experience for everybody—"

They said some things I couldn't make out, and Andre cursed and groaned as they did something to adjust his position. I stayed there, leaning against the wall, my head down, trying to fight the emotion that overwhelmed me.

CHAPTER THIRTY-ONE

I worked with Dad that fall and winter, finishing and driving the rowing shells to destinations throughout the Midwest and the South. I did a great deal of freelance writing, eventually establishing a business that I called Hurka Communications; I primarily wrote feature articles for *The Aurora Beacon News,* a large paper near our home, and local ad copy, and copy for an insurance company in Chicago.

In calls to Andre, I heard about the difficulties of his rehabilitation; he and the family had opted that he go straight home after Mass General instead of to a rehab facility, and they were regretting that lack of transition now—everything was hard, visiting nurses were coming in to help, things were rough on Peggy, pregnant and trying to take care of Andre and Cadence. Eventually, Andre made routine trips to a therapist he called "Mrs. T," at Hale Hospital in Haverhill. Her full name was Judith Tranberg, and Andre admired her forthright spirit; she had worked at Walter Reed with amputees from the Korean War, he said. Andre spoke of her, and all his physical therapists, with gratitude.

On the tenth of January, Madeleine was born and when he told me about it, I heard true joy in my friend's voice for the first time in months.

•

There was a winter day, then: February, taking the train from Aurora into Union station in the early morning darkness, dressed in my suit and overcoat, the train swaying and filled with half-sleeping businessmen and women. The vast train yards, the skyline of Chicago still shadowed as we pulled in. Everyone rising. Women in their sneakers, carrying bags over their shoulders, men with their briefcases descending ahead of me, down the train stairs, the razored lines at the napes of their necks as they bent forward, stepping onto the platform. The dim early morning cold of the station, breath in the air, then the cement sidewalks, the early morning breakfast places lit and busy, over a bridge of the Chicago River to Wacker Avenue. My shoes clicking on the cement, thousands of window lights above losing their intensity with the morning coming, that internal light disappearing into daylight. I stepped into the glass building, through revolving doors, up the elevator, bodies tight and surrounding me, rode up to the insurance company—a floor-spread of cubicles under solid overhead lamps. I worked in one of those cubicles all day, near a window with Chicago in a blue sky-winter haze below me, trying to meet the deadlines of the afternoon. I was creating "incentive programs" for agents—promising them rewards of grandfather clocks, watches, electronic back massagers, pianos—if they could sell the required number of insurance policies. A manager came out to see me; crisp tie, blue blazer. He was impressed with my writing, my efficiency: perhaps I would be interested in applying for the full-time job they had opening for a copy writer? They liked my MFA, the fact that I was creative. I would have to compete against a pool of candidates, but my chances were good. I told the manager thank you for the opportunity, I had some thinking to do, could he give me some time? *Of course, of course,* he said. He was collegiate, with a kind of practiced, friendly dignity: his face promised financial ease, calm, the beginning of a solid suburban Chicagoland life. The tone of his voice suggested that I was already on the team. Down the elevator into the February dusk, back to Union Station, to the 5:40. The train came in, the same commuters filed up the beaten rubber train stairs, the great machines glided out of the platforms and through the train yards and west, people tired in their seats, ready for home.

I could never make a life from this, I decided, my head riding on the glass, the first crowded suburbs going by: the money might eventually be good—stellar, in some advertising circles—and the life might fit some people, but I wanted to teach, or at least do something more productive with my writing, and I wanted a more active engagement with my art. I thought of the four freshman classes I'd taught at Iowa, all those young faces, those people I'd become close to. I thought of the classes I'd taught at Bradford with Andre, the faces of our students, and the light of Tupelo Pond out there. The next day I told the company manager I wanted to stay with my freelance business, thank you for the opportunity.

CHAPTER THIRTY-TWO

When the offer came from the east to do the communications for a ski area owned and run by a friend of mine, I decided on taking it. Everyone in the family was considering going east again, by that point: Chris was thinking seriously about attending school where I had, at New England College, because it had the Division I ski team; Mom and Dad spoke of getting back to the ocean and mountains, the life they'd known north of Boston—perhaps they would move farther up to a more rural area (they would soon purchase a home in Brandon, Vermont).

I drove east in September 1987, in a tan Volkswagen Rabbit that I'd bought for nine hundred dollars a few months before, after the Chevette finally quit. As soon as I came to New England and settled in—I was living at first in a small room on the mountain where I would work—I made the journey to Andre's new place. It was almost a year since I'd seen him. The modern, prefabricated home was set on a hill, a modular redwood structure with a triple zigzag of a handicapped ramp that Jeb and Young Andre had constructed leading up to the kitchen door. Leaves of poplar and birch trees shimmered on this autumn day as I came up the driveway, and I saw Andre smiling and waving at me, in his wheelchair, from the second ramp landing; beside him was Tom Brandolini, Suzanne's boyfriend. I parked where the driveway leveled out, beside Tom's car.

Andre called out "Hey buddy!" happily, when I got out.

"You look *great*," I said, and meant it: now, in this moment, he looked like himself again, in his blue Red Sox jacket, his hair a little whiter; the leaves kicked up and turned over behind him.

I took, from the passenger seat, a new copy of *Alaska Quarterly Review* with my story, "The Great White Bluesman" in it—the story I'd worked on, through tape recordings, with Andre in the summer of my junior year. I'd kept the acceptance a secret; it was my first larger publication in a quarterly and I wanted to surprise Andre with a copy of it here.

As I walked upwards, I saw Andre and Tom talking, planning: Andre had a surprise in store for me, also. He and Tom made sure the wheelchair was anchored, and then, as I came up the ramp toward them, I saw Andre working his arms and legs to stand. He and Tom had agreed, apparently, that he would manage alone. I stopped a few feet from him. It was a titanic struggle, Andre's hands and arms shaking on the wheelchair armrests, his shoulders quivering. Tom had one hand in the air behind Andre, and I watched my friend rise and stand on his prosthetic leg. Once he was stable, he held out his arms to me, laughing at his effort. I set *Alaska Quarterly Review* on the wooden railing and leaned in to carefully hug him, glad for his spirit. But, holding him, I was suddenly alarmed at his broken body. I could feel in my arms how much vitality he'd lost, how fragile his bones were, how he was shorter, and how out-of-control his muscles were.

We helped him lower back into the chair, and he rested a moment and asked me how the drive was. I said, "It's about twenty-one hours on the road, with a few stops to sleep at rest areas."

"You're working at a ski resort?" Andre said.

"In Peterborough," I said. "The owner and manager is an old friend of mine—I'll be doing his public relations."

He recovered from his exertions. I showed him the *Alaska Quarterly Review* and his face lit up. He took it and held it with reverence, smoothing his hand over the cover. He turned to my story, taking in the title, my name in print. He even smelled the pages. He said, *Congratulations, buddy. Many more to come.* It was so dry and cool in that autumn air that you felt you could lift over the valley; as we spoke, Andre kept holding on to the literary quarterly.

•

I had missed a great deal since I'd seen him—I felt this as I watched his head bent to the journal, as he turned the pages with the fingers that were so familiar to me, that brought back so many memories of Seminar D at Bradford. I had missed the long months of recovery, Andre's difficult sessions with Mrs. T at Hale Hospital (I would meet her, finally, this fall—she was tough and caring, everything Andre said she was), Peggy trying to cover all the bases: her husband's situation and nearly five-year-old Cadence and the newborn Madeleine simultaneously. The therapists still believed Andre would walk again, but I sensed, here as we spoke—still feeling the physical shock of our embrace from a few moments ago—that he never would. It was like the walk down the Massachusetts General hallway with the orthopedist, as I realized the certainty of the amputation: a faint ringing in the ears, a sensation of a harsh reality setting in; a truth you couldn't turn away from. I felt myself putting on a brave smile for my friend, as we joked and caught up on our lives. He asked about faculty he knew at Iowa and what writing and working in the Chicago area were like, and he spoke as always of the Red Sox, their chances in the upcoming season. I knew that Peggy and Andre's marriage had started to fall apart under all the strain of the last year—we didn't bring it up, now, but I'd heard fragments of this in a few of our recent phone calls, that things had been rocky for them even before the accident. I didn't exactly know how they were doing now. I believe at this time they were already not living together and sharing a kind of informal joint custody of the children.

Family and friends were pitching in to ease things for Andre: building ramps into the living room and onto the sun decks; helping rearrange the house for a man in a wheelchair; cooking, cleaning, helping watch the children when they were with him. There had been important help from the literary community, also. In February and March, John Irving and Kurt Vonnegut had organized a series of readings to aid Andre financially; at the Charles Hotel in Cambridge, through five Sunday afternoons, a march of luminaries showed up on behalf of their mutual friend: Ann Beattie, E.L. Doctorow, Gail Godwin, Stephen King, Tim O'Brien, Jayne Anne Phillips, John Updike, and Richard Yates. Together, they'd raised eighty-six thousand dollars for Andre to help with the bills in this tough time.

CHAPTER THIRTY-THREE

Temple Mountain was located in a thickly-wooded area just off Route 101 in Peterborough. All through that fall I wrote press releases and took photographs designed to increase the visibility of the ski area. I wrote about the fifty-year history of the place, the testing of the chairlifts, and the current preparations for the season: the clearing of trails and repairs to the ski lodge. I got us mentioned frequently in places like *The Monadnock Ledger* and *The Manchester Union Leader,* and less often in *The Boston Globe* and on local television and radio shows. I tried to get as much free press as possible. The ski area was a little off the beaten track for the Boston ski crowd, which was more likely to go up to the northern mountains of New Hampshire on Route 93. I had long discussions with Sandy Eneguess, the manager and owner of the area (when I'd been a teenager Sandy was a top, nationally-ranked ski and canoe racer, and I'd always looked up to him); Sandy reasoned that if we could alert Boston that there was a viable alternative to some of the better-known ski areas, and that it was not far away, we could have a strong season. Our efforts met with success: as the snow began to fall and the slopes turned white the crowds came in, jamming the parking lot. My office was at the end of a boardwalk at the bottom of the mountain, the last in a row of ramshackle offices each the size of a large closet. I had an electric typewriter there, packages of fresh paper, and a binder full of public relations ideas for the ski industry. A phone was on my small desk, and an electric heater at my feet. A window looked out onto the bottom slopes of the mountain. I didn't ski too much. I worked long hours on the advertising and intermountain communications and went home to my apartment in Jaffrey, the next town over, a place with warped floors and maddingly knocking radiators. Often I was exhausted, but I kept up my fiction writing; I have memories of getting home late in the evenings, having take-out dinners of steak and cheese grinders or meatball subs, then working from eight until midnight, sometimes longer, at the built-in linoleum island kitchen counter, the writing of the stories bringing me to life as if I wasn't tired at all.

Sometime during that snowy New Hampshire winter, I got word from Andre that a friend of his, Don Hendrie Jr., the director of the MFA program at the University of Alabama, had nominated "The Great White Bluesman" for a Pushcart Prize. The story didn't win, but just being in the running gave me a much-needed shot of confidence.

CHAPTER THIRTY-FOUR

On my days off, I drove through that late autumn and winter of 1987-88, the trees by the sides of Highway 101 at first stripped of their leaves, then snow falling and melting on the tar, gathering dirty white at the sides of the highway—then into the winter of storms, to help Andre care for his children. He organized his friends and some paid helpers in a schedule that he planned well ahead of time, and in addition to being one of those friends he could count on, I told him if I was free I would always fill in if someone else couldn't make it. I was there often. Andre was out to prove, I think, that even in his crippled condition and as a single man he could handle the responsibilities of fatherhood. He was beginning to get around more proficiently in the wheelchair, though still adjusting, constantly, to his new reality. I spent as much time there as I could, wondering how this would all play out; I cooked for the kids, read them stories, drew pictures with them, watched movies and television shows with them and Andre. I tried to offer the children a calm, predictable presence. Many times, I would be there for an afternoon and evening, then spend the night on the couch and give them breakfast the next day, and be on the road again north.

The divorce happened later that winter. The court gave Andre shared but not physical custody of his daughters. At the dissolution of his marriage, the official upending of the family, Andre wrestled with persistent feelings of loss, failure, and sorrow.

CHAPTER THIRTY-FIVE

To live as an amputee confined to a wheelchair is to enter an entirely different physical world. In dreams, Andre would tell me, you have your full body, but you wake to the reality of this new one, the brokenness of it ("I use the word *crippled,*" Andre told me. "I'm not *physically challenged.* That's just a bullshit phrase to make somebody—some outsider—feel better. I'm *crippled.* It's a good, accurate word.").

He told me: there is often a fatigue you feel, right from your waking hour, knowing the emotional and physical fight that you'll face in your day. A urinal is always nearby, hanging on the bed or on your wheelchair; you rise and transfer to the wheelchair and wheel down the hallway and it takes some maneuvering, a grasping of your hands beneath the atrophied calf and lifting up of your leg, to make the corner into the bathroom; then some tight jockeying to get onto the toilet for a bowel movement. It is an effort, a reach, to wash your hands, to brush your teeth. When you want to wash your body, you slide onto the plastic seat set in the shower, bracing yourself with the handicapped rail on the wall. Andre's bathroom was narrow, tight. Things he took for granted before—toiletries, lotions, medications—were set within arm's length. This was true of the kitchen and more expansive dining area as well; eventually, he had so many medications that there was a drawer dedicated to them within easy reach in the dining room. Pots and pans, utensils and plates all were above this in the same hutch, easily accessible. When Andre needed to get hold of something beyond the scope of his arms, he used a "grabber"—an extended metal piece with a trigger and a clutching mechanism at the end to firmly secure things with. *All of your actions,* Andre told me one morning, *take three times as long—washing, getting dressed, cooking.* But I saw his frustration give way, in time, to a new patience with himself and the world around him—a tolerance.

•

His art also demanded change. He was working on a story about a character named Robert Townsend, a retired Marine colonel. "I realize that in my writing I'm facing something psychological," he told me over a lunch he'd made of his favorite rice and beans *("peasant food,"* he called it, proudly). "I'm seeing the world from a new perspective, from the level of the wheelchair. I was having trouble getting into my character's *soul,* because I can't see anything now from the perspective of a man standing; so, I finally decided to break *his* legs. Then the story started moving."

In "The Colonel's Wife," it is winter, and Robert Townsend is recovering from a riding accident: a horse has fallen on his legs. Both legs are in full casts and when he returns from the hospital, he is set up temporarily "downstairs in the living room on a hospital bed whose ends he could raise or lower, to evade pain. The bed was narrow, and his golden-haired wife, Lydia, slept upstairs."

Lydia is thoughtful, loving, and attentive to her severely injured husband. She empties his urinal, helps him in and out of his wheelchair and onto a commode near his bed. She tells him not to be embarrassed, "but his stench and filth, the intimacy of her hands and voice, slapped his soul with a wet cloth." Robert fights his physical pain with Demerol, Percodan; his spiritual pain, which he is mostly quiet about, is the greater trial. He fears fire, snowstorms, electrical shutdowns. He fears for his future with Lydia.

One day he watches his wife as she comes through the door from shopping, and from the light, the distraction in her face, he realizes she has another lover.

He says nothing. But that night, thinking of the hopelessness of his situation, Colonel Townsend has a breakdown. He is startled from his weeping by his wife, holding his hands: *"then her voice was in his heart. 'Bob,' she said. 'Bobby.'"* Throughout the long night, Robert and Lydia Townsend confess their failings, their infidelities, to one another—it is not her first affair, she tells him; he was with prostitutes in Japan, Hong Kong, Vietnam—some of this she has guessed at. Now, watching his wife's emotional face as she speaks, Robert experiences Lydia's mortality, imagining her at the start of life, a "golden-haired child ... then he saw her gray and thin and dying in pain."

At the end of the story the two have grown closer. "I'm glad that damned horse fell on me," Robert tells his wife. "It made me lie still in one place and look at you."

•

He was giving me copies of his stories and essays as he wrote them. Sometimes I took his original manuscripts to a copy center in Newburyport and ran them off myself, reserving one copy to read when I got home later. I have a thick stack of these pages here in New Hampshire where I'm writing, thirty manuscripts from the period after his accident. Many are inscribed to me—*for Joe, with love,* they say, with the dates that these final drafts were completed.

At first there were long gaps of time—months, sometimes—in which Andre simply could not write. Then the words came more steadily. A new dimension unfolded in the passages Andre composed now, mirroring his physical journey. The experience of brokenness, both of his body and family, made him contend with a powerful grief that sometimes nearly consumed him. Ultimately, because his spirit was a big one and he had to survive, grief and fear led to forgiveness and redemption, both on the page and in life. *Fear is a ghost;* he wrote, in a story called "Woman on a Plane": *embrace your fear, and all you'll see in your arms is yourself.*

•

A number of times, if the children had gone home with Peggy late and I spent the night at the house—Sundays I had off and Mondays I was only due back to the mountain at one in the afternoon—I woke up to write in the living room while Andre worked in his bedroom, at the wooden desk Young Andre had built him that looked onto the deck and the valley. He had his record books there, a rack of pipes, his pens; on the wall to the right was the only plaque of appreciation to him I ever saw on any of his walls—for his readings and fund-raising efforts for wounded veterans. We often compared notes afterward. Andre was exploring what he called "vertical" writing then: "I used to try and get a certain word count for the day," he said. "Now I'm concentrating on getting five to seven lines, on staying with those sentences until they are as thorough as I can make them. I almost always write more, but the point is I'm thinking vertically rather than horizontally. Slowing things way down, doing fewer drafts."

The "vertical" philosophy took root in him. Much later, on a January evening in 1994 when I was a college professor and living in Newburyport, Andre called and wanted me to come over and hear him read a story he'd finished that afternoon. I drove the twenty minutes down Highway 113, turned in after the green at West Newbury, over the bridge spanning the Merrimack in last winter light. The sun had completely fallen when I arrived and the floor-to-ceiling window behind Andre's desk was a glossy black; I could see, faintly, snow on the railings of the deck out there. He rolled over to me in his wheelchair with his record book in his lap, and behind him was his clear reflection—his head and shoulders and the back of his wheelchair—as he raised the record book to read. He adjusted his reading glasses on his nose. "*The murder began someplace in her heart,*" he read, "*a place she had never been: it was like a shadowed mountain pass, then a brilliant plain. The plain drew her. She stepped into it one night in bed with the sixteen-year-old boy.*"

"The Last Moon" goes directly into the dark soul of a twenty-five-year-old unnamed high school counselor; initially, she is in bed with one of her advisees, manipulating the boy into murdering her husband. The story is based loosely on the Pamela Smart case in New Hampshire; Smart had recently been imprisoned, and she was still much in the news. In Andre's story, the counselor discovers, as the reader discovers, that she is not so much drawn to the insurance money her husband's murder will net her, or to taking the boy's virginity, his "frenzy"; the real attraction is to the overall evil she alone puts into momentum. Her husband is a basketball coach at the high school who routinely leaves work late: at the end of this brief tale, the counselor sits in a café drinking tea, imagining the boy hiding in her husband's car, at that moment, with a gun. Her husband walking through the parking lot "under his last moon." The boy will do it, she knows, for she has set him "ablaze."

When Andre had finished reading, I told him the story was stunning—I felt it was one of his best. We talked about what had driven the work.

"I was guided by the question," he said, rolling over to me and handing me the record book (I always liked looking over his stories in his original handwriting), "—what would it be like to have arranged the killing of your husband, and then make love to him?" A passage near the end of the piece had given him his answer: *"and in her heart then he was dead and she was in motion; and for the next eleven days and twelve nights she heard and saw him from that distance, and she made love with him because it was dazzling."*

I looked at the handwriting below me carefully, remembering when Andre had first told me about his idea of the "vertical" writing; it occurred to me then that the patience he'd had to learn because of his crippling had been a critical element of this. I was struck, looking at the prose below me, by the fact that there were precious few corrections, as if something were dictating the story to the author.

CHAPTER THIRTY-SIX

Thursday nights in those years after the accident, Andre's steep driveway was routinely lined with the cars of writers: Hondas, rusting Toyotas, Volkswagens. One spring evening I parked my Volkswagen where I could; it was exceptionally warm, snow melting at the sides of the driveway. Andre had run this free workshop since before the accident, and inside there was a lot of smoking, a lot of conversing between people, ten or twelve of us altogether who had come in from all over the Boston area. I went through the kitchen and into the dining room and there was Andre sitting happily, his forearms leaning on the armrests of his wheelchair, his eyes frankly delighted with female company, with women standing just far enough away that he didn't need to crane his neck; they looked lovely. A woman was speaking to him now, her bare legs crossed at the ankles as she stood with a bottle of Perrier in her hands. Then Andre was nodding and speaking, and she was considering something he was saying, her head tilting toward him, and he caught my eye and there was his instant humor, he knew that *I* knew how a woman could make him swoon.

"Hey, buddy," he said, all of them turning to me.

Andre's home, amidst the smoke, was decorated with finger paintings by his girls on the hallway walls (I thought, walking down to put my coat on the pile in Andre's bedroom, of how Peggy was probably disturbed by this, another example of Andre's flagrant permissiveness); in the bedroom there was a photograph of Andre with his Marine unit, looking trim and stone-faced, and there was a Marine sword on the wall, above cubicles of his roughly-folded clothes; back in the dining room and living room area of the home were posters: a small rectangle of calligraphy quoting William James about the dignity of poverty; a large photograph of Walt Whitman, a side-shot of the poet in older age with his massive white beard, his words italicized: *We have frequently printed the word Democracy. Yet I cannot too often repeat that it is a word the real gist of which still sleeps, quite unawakened* ... There were posters of Andre's heroes: Mahatma Gandhi and Martin Luther King and Mother Teresa. The windows looked out over the valley, pink in the last moments of light, and you thought of the summer days ahead, baseball, green lawns, ocean. Andre rolled down the ramp, finally calling everyone to order. We all sat around him, on the couch, on chairs and benches. Usually we got through two stories a night, the authors reading aloud, the rest of us, like Andre, listening with our eyes closed. We would have animated, detailed discussions afterward. Most of the writers were enormously productive in this arrangement; Christopher Tilghman wrote some of his collection of his award-winning *In a Father's Place* in this workshop; Edie Clarke, the editor of *Yankee Magazine,* read us long passages from *The Place He Made,* about her late husband, Paul, and his battle with cancer. Jessica Treadway always struck me as the most gifted of all of us. Some of the stories she produced in the workshop would become part of her excellent collection called *Absent Without Leave.*

Andre gave us his time, his wise counsel, his patience. He was unfailingly generous. When one workshop writer needed tuition money for college, he quietly paid her bills, and would not accept repayment. He was constantly on the phone with workshop members, listening to the problems of their lives, often calling you back to bring up another idea he'd had that might help, suggesting there was a book in his own library that addressed this, and you should pick it up the next time you swung by. He came into the workshop one night with a stack of hardcopies on his lap which he passed out—he'd gotten this for us, this was something we must read, he told us. I looked down at my new, glossy copy of Annie Dillard's *The Writing Life.*

His heart was as open to strangers, especially to those less fortunate. I once saw him write out a check for five hundred dollars for a homeless man and say *Merry Christmas.* He gave routinely to a Catholic homeless shelter in New York City—he never told me how much, but I suspect the amount was substantial. After the gift of the Dillard book I hoped his bank account could survive his generosity—I calculated that bill to be nearly two hundred dollars—and told him so privately. *I hope God will mark this sparrow,* he told me, smiling. But he kept on giving.

Jim McPherson, who had once won the MacArthur "Genius" Grant along with the Pulitzer, called me one night in 1988.

He said, "Joe, I understand that Andre is selling his original manuscripts for income. Do you know if this is true?"

I said it was—Andre was selling the record books he wrote in to wealthy patrons and to Louisiana State University, which was steadily collecting his papers.

"*All* right," Jim said, in his quiet way. "All right. Thank you, Joe."

Andre won the MacArthur, roughly $310,000, that year. I couldn't be sure, but I thought Jim might've been the angel who set the miracle in motion. Andre described the award to me as a blessing from God.

CHAPTER THIRTY-SEVEN

Jim called me in 1989, when I was searching for teaching jobs anywhere in New England. I didn't want to do any more public relations writing, but it was already August now. I'd gone through seventeen leads at various colleges throughout the area; I had a few offers, I told Jim, but most were adjunct jobs with very low pay and little else—no health care, nothing in the way of retirement incentives. I would have to string about three jobs together to make any kind of living at all. Jim told me there was a job opening at Tufts University teaching freshman English, and sent me to an interview there with Alan Leibowitz, his old Harvard professor and now the head of the Tufts English department, and Linda Bamber, head of the freshman writing program. Tufts offered a yearly contract, plus a retirement account, in addition to a traditional CREF account, in which the school put funds away for you annually. You had your choice of a number of medical plans. It was part-time work, but glorified part-time, considered a "lectureship," and much in demand.

In East Hall, a brick structure dating back to the Civil War, I sat in my best blue suit with Linda and Alan, trying to answer their questions thoroughly, hoping I was making a good impression. Afterward, Alan took me for a walk on campus, a warm, breezy day, telling me I had the job if I wanted it. After my months of worry—of whether I would have a teaching job to show by fall—this was breathtaking; I thought about what a gift Jim had given me, and Alan smoked his pipe and philosophized about teaching. We walked along the quad beneath the trees of summer, and students were spread all over, reading and chatting on the lawn. *It's really the last honest job, teaching,* Alan told me. Linda and Alan would become good friends of mine in the close Tufts faculty.

Jim also sent me, that August, to interview with DeWitt Henry, who ran the WLP (Writing, Literature, and Publishing) division at Emerson College on Beacon Street in Boston. DeWitt was a founder and editor of the famous *Ploughshares* literary quarterly, and a long-time friend of Jim and Andre's and eventually of mine; he asked me to teach one section of creative writing.

So, because of Jim McPherson's kindness, and because of the work Andre had patiently guided me into, I was suddenly set into a life of teaching: I would have yearly contracts with both schools. Three days a week that fall I commuted to Medford and parked near my office in Lane Hall, a small corner room just up a set of stairs from some huge ancient imprints of dinosaur feet and a classroom where models posed for art students. I arranged my papers and went into my day. I taught in older buildings like Braker and Eaton Hall, built sometime in the early nineteen-hundreds—my students were consistently bright freshmen, remarkably thorough. I quickly settled into having a familiar sense of purpose around these young people. Two of the late afternoons of the week I drove over the 93 deck to Boston, parking on Beacon Street, climbing up the gritty wooden stairways of an old townhouse that Emerson then owned, to meet students who aspired to writing, painting, acting, some en route to becoming top journalists and broadcasters. I found myself channeling Andre in these classes, relying even on his mannerisms sometimes, thinking of how he would approach a discussion or student situation. I always liked driving home from Boston at a later hour, the city sparkling as you wound onto 95 North heading to Newburyport, and I often thought of that first day of meeting Andre, how I'd considered this new direction in life, how I'd looked at these lights of the city as I left my audition.

CHAPTER THIRTY-EIGHT

There is a point for an amputee, after a long recovery, when you buy a car that accommodates you, with hand controls, and a large metal box on top for carrying the wheelchair. You roll down the outdoor handicapped ramp, zigzagging to the flat part of the driveway, slowing the chair by braking steadily with your hands, your leather gloves on the wheels. You glide down to your maroon Toyota Celica. You open the door, brake the chair beside it, remove an armrest, and transfer your body with a transfer board to the driver's seat. Rip the Velcro pad on the wheelchair seat out, toss it to the passenger side of the vehicle, take the other armrest and the leg brace off the chair, put them in the car as well. Press a button beneath the driver's seat and the wheelchair box above cracks open and a cable comes down with a rod that slides through the middle of the wheelchair seat; you send the chair upwards; it folds over the rod, raises, tilts and slips sideways into the box and the box closes with a *thump*. Or if a friend is driving, he takes you to the passenger side, helps you slide into the passenger seat, and takes the chair around himself to the driver's side, goes through the procedure himself.

Everywhere you go as an amputee, as you get out of the car, as you roll over a sidewalk, people stare. Or try not to stare. An amputated body is out of symmetry, and a lack of symmetry makes people think of mortality. Many turn their eyes away.

If you are the caretaker of a man in a wheelchair, you roll him over the surface of the earth; you watch ahead for obstacles. Brick sidewalks roll unevenly, sometimes jerk; tar has a rugged feel to it. Smooth white cement seems to run best, the kind found on many modern handicapped ramps. Frequently, the transition from a road crossing to a sidewalk has a jarring lip to it, and when you see one coming up you are better off turning the chair around and taking your friend over it backwards. Children stare in honest horror at your friend's missing leg; parents quickly direct them to avert their eyes. Adults often don't know what to say when you are communicating with them; a shopkeeper shifts his eyes from Andre, asks what accommodations your friend needs. You want to say, *Why don't you ask him? He's right here in front of you.*

•

We drove everywhere together, first in the old Volkswagen, and then in a new Honda Civic that I bought, and in Andre's handicapped-equipped Toyota when he purchased it. We made a tradition of shopping together at Christmas. That first holiday season that I was back in New England, we went to Service Merchandise in Salem, New Hampshire; Andre bought way too much for his family—we made the journey in the Volkswagen, and on the way home we could barely fit everything in. We went to a specialized clothing shop in Newburyport for more presents (tough brick sidewalks), and a candle-store there, and a bookstore where I carried bags of Andre's gifts. Next to a Christmas tree farm where we got into an argument over, of all things, the space program.

"That money should be going to the poor," Andre said, angrily, as we wobbled through the rows of Christmas trees.

"But don't you see, buddy," I said, "how much mankind benefits from exploration? The inspiration for young people?"

"Eating comes first," Andre said. "A lot of families could be fed for all that fucking money we're blowing up in space."

In summers, we took the kids to an ice-cream stand nearby, and often to a llama farm just down Broadway. In autumn, the two of us met for exercise at parking lot 1 in the Plum Island Wildlife Sanctuary, Andre rolling himself and me walking, all around the large lot and up the boardwalk to the sea.

We drove to doctor's appointments in Boston and Haverhill and Andover, and eventually to readings Andre had at local libraries and schools and colleges and then farther away, in southern and western New England. We journeyed to the Screening Room in Newburyport with the Bailey Girls, a group of teenaged survivors of domestic violence who, through a program with the Catholic church, Andre met with once a week either to read stories with or see movies with. One late summer afternoon Andre took this group to see *Othello* and invited me along. It was moving to see how these young women with so many strikes against them took ownership of Andre afterward, insisting on taking over the wheelchair, taking turns pushing him over the brick walkways of the seaport, debating loudly amongst one another and with Andre about the meanings of the play.

Andre and I went sometimes twice a week to Showcase Cinemas in Lawrence. There, with the huge screens and crystal-clear sound, Andre could lose himself in other stories, in the work of other creative people. We had a habit of leaving the theater only after all the credits had rolled: Andre wanted to take in all the names of those who had worked on the film. We were always the last ones in these vast, popcorn-strewn spaces. We saw *Goodfellas* and *The Fabulous Baker Boys* and *Field of Dreams* and *Batman*. We saw *Dances With Wolves* and *JFK* and *Good Will Hunting* and *Jurassic Park.* Sometimes we went to the films with a collection of other writers, sometimes just the two of us setting off down 495 to the cineplex. "Movies are great because you can do your work early in the day and then go into this other world and get away from the monster in your head," Andre told me, as we waited for the start of *Goldeneye.* He sat beside me, in the aisle, toward the front of the theatre. He had his traditional popcorn, a Diet Coke, a large box of Goobers. The trailers ended and the lights went down and in that darkness Andre watched quietly beside me, his hands folded on his abdomen, the urinal clipped to the lower right side of the chair. Pierce Brosnan above us was in a tense standoff in his first outing as James Bond, and I felt my friend escape his work for a brief couple of hours, escape his tired, aching legs.

•

There were infections of Andre's amputated leg, journeys to Boston. One summer day at Massachusetts General we had an extraordinarily attractive nurse tending to us. She seemed receptive to my humor at first, and then I had to leave the room to talk with a doctor. When I returned my efforts at charm were met with a cool professionalism.

"I don't know what I did wrong," I said, rolling Andre before me out of the building. "I thought at first she might be interested."

Andre put on his best southern-hick accent. "I told her you were a *homosexual.* I said, Joey's a nice boy, but he don't like *women.*"

"You would, wouldn't you?"

"Just looking out for my pal Joey."

In the parking garage I got Andre into the passenger seat and, on the driver's side, put the chair into the rooftop storage and got behind the wheel. I started the car: you touched the brake once and the Toyota reverted to regular clutch-brake-accelerator operation. We drove out into the sun and I put the visor down and turned onto Storrow Drive; it was a little past noon and traffic was light. Sails on the Charles River were bright on the water, and people ran on the jogging paths. The Esplanade waited for an evening orchestra. Andre rested his legs in the passenger seat beside me, liberated momentarily from the tension, the worry, of his medical situation, and our banter went on. It helped get our thoughts away from the tougher things: most of these visits were, for Andre, an exercise in endurance.

CHAPTER THIRTY-NINE

Opening day at Fenway Park had always been a kind of religious journey for Andre: in the past, teaching at Bradford, he'd cancelled classes on that day each year and gone with close friends to the Red Sox opener. At the opener to the second season after Andre's accident, 1988, the writer Dennis Lehane drove up to the house with official Fenway hot dogs; Dennis fried the hot dogs in one of Andre's skillets and the three of us ate them with buns and potato chips that Dennis had brought and Cokes and watched the game.

Then there was a day, I think sometime during that same summer, as Andre was steadily regaining his mobility, that he returned to Fenway Park for the first time since the accident. We got there early, but the crowd was already packed in, the emerald green of the field, the Green Monster—always magical sights—before us. Andre flung up his hands. "All *right*," he said.

I asked some guys to help me get him down over the broad gray steps toward the Red Sox dugout—we had a handicapped spot and a seat just behind it—and they jammed cigarettes in their mouths and quickly complied. A booming announcement came through the Fenway loudspeaker system then: "*Fenway Park welcomes back New England writer Andre*

Dubus, here for the first time since the accident that left him in a wheelchair. Good luck with your recovery, Andre, and welcome!" A friend of Andre's with connections to the Red Sox organization had alerted the announcer to Andre's arrival; Andre's eyes widened with surprise and he flung up his hands again in joy and gave high-fives all around. Everywhere you looked there were cheering faces.

•

Cambridge: a cool summer night; some years on. There was a well-known poet, a beautiful woman; Andre was wild about her. He fell in love often (the wheelchair wasn't much of a hindrance, despite some initial self-consciousness) but she was a stand-out even among his many erotic yearnings: an artist of wisdom and deep talent, with blond, close-cropped hair and bright-green eyes and a disposition that made her seem perpetually accessible, someone people were always glad to be with. She had invited Andre and me to a gathering at a Chinese restaurant, a celebration of some kind—perhaps a birthday. She liked Andre but I'm not sure why she wanted him there. Clearly she felt the heat of his interest but she was much younger and the infatuation wasn't, I could tell, mutual; perhaps she had the instinct that, if he observed her with her friends, Andre's interest in romance would somehow dissipate.

Everyone was smoking; we were introduced all around. Our new acquaintances were clever, their opinions (except for the poet and one or two of the others—a strange imbalance) almost always sarcastic, witty. There was a game going on which I think I'm remembering correctly: one person would make up a word, along with a definition they kept secret—the word would be announced, clues distributed, and the rest of us would have to guess at what the word meant. There was much dark humor, sly innuendo, much hinting at debauchery. One of these words was announced; the Latin-sounding *propagosanita* clued us in on the fact that it would be defined as something akin to *promoting sanity, reason,* "something you could not expect from your average Cro-Magnon pro-lifer," the clue-giver, a swarthy male academic, said, to great laughter.

I saw something drift through my Catholic friend's eyes, the charge of social play being replaced by more somber emotion. It wasn't long before we made our excuses and were rolling over the gray-brown cobblestones of Harvard Square. There was a streetlight behind us and Andre was quiet, his head bent, our shadows long and dark before us.

"Most of the time I was pretty lost in there," I said. "All that wit. I'm just not that fast. I felt dumb."

"I felt dumb in there, too," Andre said. He looked up: an intersection in the distance was busy like a riotous circus. "But they certainly were impressed with themselves."

I said something about my philosophy that relentless sarcasm was the refuge of the mediocre; Andre nodded and gave a sound of affirmation, but he was quiet, thoughtful, recovering from the odd evening. He could sometimes gently scorn the "02138" (Cambridge) writers, and here we'd had an example of why—a group who congratulated themselves a little too much and didn't seem to turn their eyes to the world or concern themselves with the sensitivities of others. Most writers and academics at least knew who Andre was and would have known about his faith; perhaps, I was thinking, that Cro-Magnon bit had been a dig at him. But no, I decided, more likely the clever male academic and his friends were oblivious.

We had parked in the Charles Hotel. The lights were bright around us now, making ovals on the brick walls of Cambridge, and a group of students went by, full of chatter. The cobblestones gave way to smoother tar.

"I don't think she's like the others, though, somehow," I said. "Really."

"No, I don't think so either. She's more humane. I think that display surprised her a little bit too."

A few days later we were driving to Fenway Park, Andre behind the wheel of the Toyota. It was a game that we'd been talking about for weeks: Nolan Ryan of the Rangers would be in a dual against Roger Clemens, the ace pitcher of the Red Sox. A friend of Andre's, who worked for the local television station, WBZ, had skybox seats waiting for us. We got snarled in traffic approaching Boston University. Then we couldn't find a parking space—handicapped or otherwise—anywhere around Fenway, even when a well-meaning cop searched for us. We finally gave up and headed home over the bridge of Massachusetts Avenue toward Cambridge. We shook our heads at our ill-fortune.

"We're having quite a week," I said.

"There's one good thing," Andre said, glancing right. He pointed to a row of townhouses that came up quickly. He grinned. "That's where she lives. At least I get to show you that."

"I know the place well, buddy," I said, as casually as I could. "I left there just this morning."

Andre was quiet a moment, rocking in the aftermath of my pronouncement. "Oh," he said. "You *are* an asshole."

CHAPTER FORTY

Andre's relationships with women were complex, and often a mystery to me. Women, friends of mine, writers—some of whom had dated Andre—told me he was still very much a man of the fifties. That in virtually any friendship with a woman Andre tested the romantic—the sexual—waters, that you always came to those crossroads with him but once it was clear that an intimate relationship was *not* going to happen, he switched quickly to a friendship that was genuine and lasting. Women constantly told me how interesting he was to be around, how constantly curious he was. "Truly, one of the best conversationalists in the world," one told me.

On the afternoon of his first real date after the accident—I can't remember precisely when this was or who the woman was—I went with Andre to a car wash in nearby Amesbury to help him vacuum out and clean and wash the Toyota so it would be presentable. I got Andre out of the passenger seat and I went at the driver's side with the nozzle, then handed the hose to Andre in his wheelchair and he bent forward and cleaned the seat and floor as best he could on his side. I cleaned the vinyl dashboard and took the vacuum hose back and did the back seats and floor. We sat through the car wash, remarking at how strange the machinery moving around us made us feel, the water plunging over the windshield like we were under a waterfall. We drove back to Andre's home and I pushed Andre up the ramp and told him I would leave him so that he could get ready and wished him luck. He told me, laughing at himself a little, that he was nervous—he hoped he wouldn't screw this up or embarrass himself. "Everything is supposed to be accessible at this restaurant, but I hope there are no glitches. I shouldn't be embarrassed, but I know I would be if something gets fucked up."

I said I thought it would be fine, that from the way he described his date, it sounded like she was understanding and would be a help in any tough situation. The first shadows of evening, of forests and houses, were on the turnpike as I wound my way home on 113. I was nervous for my friend—it took effort and courage to gear up for a first date even in normal circumstances, and Andre had to face so much extra; well, at least his car was *squared away,* as he would put it. I hoped things would go well.

I met up with Andre and a group of friends the next night in the bar at Ten Centre Street in Newburyport, including Jack Herlihy (Jack had recently started renting a part of Andre's house, and was helping Andre with the kids, rides, cooking) and Jeb and Young Andre and Young Andre's lifelong friend, Bill Cantwell, all of us eager for a debriefing.

"She was beautiful," Andre told us. "I was so nervous, I pretty much agreed with everything she said. I lied a *lot.* At one point she told me she didn't like reading magazines and I said 'Yep—'" he made a motion of his nose growing like Pinocchio— "'I don't like them, either.'"

We all laughed. I was relieved that this milestone had come and gone without incident. I imagined the woman as Andre had described her: brown-haired, green-eyed, very attractive, sitting in candlelight. Absorbed in Andre's big spirit. They weren't kindred souls, and it didn't seem that a great romance was blooming, but he was getting back in the world, moment by moment.

•

It was when he fell deeper into relationships that a consistent troubled theme seemed often to crop up. I thought it was rooted in his lifelong training in fiction: his ability to discover metaphors even in the smallest things. It was in a kind of scrutiny of the Other, putting her habits and lifestyle under a microscope. He wanted to know why you did things the way you did: he wanted to know what your actions meant. With women, sometimes, his observations seemed far too acute and unrelenting. And accurate: usually Andre's instincts about people were on-target ("paranoid people are usually right," Andre would say). One woman he had a great interest in and who came from wealthy circumstances told him, on one of their dates, that her family had a private beach on the New England coast. Andre at heart believed that the public should have access to everything, and I knew when he first mentioned that private beach to me, in a phone call, that the relationship was doomed. It was a deal-breaker: a fact that seemed to contain dark clues to the woman's character—that she might be, deep beneath her confessed liberal sympathies, an elitist. I watched, over a week-long period, as Andre came to this certainty. "Why the fuck should *anybody* have a private beach?" he asked me, in one of our many ruminations over the subject. By the end of that week, the budding relationship was done.

Still, despite this—the tumble of emotions his scrutiny often caused—he was an optimist about the joining of the sexes, the moving on of the species. He came back from an annual summer gathering with his extended family at a cabin in New Hampshire once, revitalized. "I realized, looking at everyone, these generations, that this whole thing, everything—" he spread his arms with reverence to indicate the enormity of humanity "—all of it is about fucking."

•

I pull a book out of my library here in New Hampshire. It is by Michael Blumenthal, a slim volume of poetry called *Against Romance,* with a Pierre Bonnard piece, *The Terrace,* illustrating the cover. Andre, Suzanne, and the children gave the book to me for my twenty-seventh birthday, a time when I was working at the ski area and driving down to help watch the kids. In Blumenthal's poem, "The Dangers of Metaphor," the poet outlines the progression of human romance—moving from rainbows to stark reality. The poem makes me think of some of Andre's relationships with women:

there are dangers in this, this beginning
with something as heavenly
as a rainbow. So I wait,
holding you up again each day
against a bleaker sky
and you become, this way,
less transparent, less embellished
by the numinous, but more real.
Last night there were no stars anywhere
and, today, desire's prism
held against the sky

yields only a pure white. In fact,
each day the sky falls
a bit closer to you, merciful
as a guillotine,
keeping you earthbound, flawed—
a human thing only another human thing could love.

CHAPTER FORTY-ONE

One cold January night, coming out of Showcase Cinemas, we saw a homeless vet pushing his grocery cart of belongings across the vast, mostly empty parking lot. It was dead freezing, papers blowing across the dry pavement: the lot must have had all of seven cars in it. There were steady gusts, a bone-chilling breeze. We sat in the Toyota, Andre starting it up, putting the heat on, and couldn't figure out how anyone could take that cold. The veteran was African-American and wore a green canvas military coat with sergeant's stripes. He had on jeans, boots, a few black watch caps, torn leather gloves. Slowly he made his way across the huge, empty parking lot, toward the cinema doors. His figure moved across that chrome and neon. The veteran parked the cart by a window and walked inside.

"How the hell does he live out here in a night like this?" I said.

"I don't know, man," Andre said. "I can't even imagine it."

It was Andre's idea to put our money together and buy the man as many gift-tickets as possible so that he could at least go into the theatre and warm up for an extended time whenever he wanted. Between the two of us we had enough cash to buy eight tickets; Andre stayed in the car and I went inside to the ticket counter, and then in the cinema complex with its sky-blue walls and buttered popcorn and vacuum smells I found the veteran sitting, unobtrusively, on a bench beneath a stairway. You had the sense that the man was adept at being unobtrusive. The wall behind him was decorated with bits of famous American speeches and writings. I caught a few lines from George Washington's famous, sharp response to businessmen who had urged him to seize power and become a king.

The veteran was probably in his mid-sixties, his face bleached from the cold. His eyes were a little watery, but steady, focused. I introduced myself. He gave a slight nod of hello and I explained Andre's idea and he looked at the tickets I held out, not understanding, at first, what I was offering. He was still dealing with recovering from the chill. Then it registered on him, and he smiled a little and shook his head.

"I'm grateful to you and your friend, son," he said. "But I can't take these from you. I don't accept charity."

I was at a loss for what to say. I knew that if I were in this man's position, I would accept any reasonable help that came my way. I was a little disturbed by his stubbornness. I wondered if the endless cold—we'd had a long snap of it—had injured his thinking, his ability to reason. I had the thought that if I was stuck in the cold for any extended period, I too could become crazy. Any human being could.

I sat with the veteran. I saw Andre out there in the car. We were here, on the edge of Lawrence, where gangs ran with their violence while honorable men like this shivered in the winter—and I wondered when he would be robbed of his few possessions, of that grocery cart I could see here through the glass; if he would be beaten in such a moment of violence, killed. I had a desperate sense that the tickets I held in my hand could somehow save this man; also, selfishly, I did not want to return to Andre and have to report that I'd failed in my efforts.

I tried to tell the homeless vet, gently, that if it were me, I would take the tickets, that at some point it might be just the relief he needed, that it would mean a lot to us if he took them. He just smiled and kept shaking his head. "I survived the cold in Korea, son. I can survive this."

Back at the car, I opened the passenger side door and flopped in the seat. Andre was looking at me expectantly, the Toyota humming with warmth. I held the tickets up.

"I tried everything," I said. "He wouldn't take them."

Andre grimaced, *"Shit."* He tapped the steering wheel with his fist. He looked at the theatre, the man now coming out again after his respite, taking up his grocery cart again and moving into the shadows of the building. Andre raised his chin, his beard rising a little, a sign of resignation.

"Too proud."

"He told me he fought in Korea."

"Poor guy."

"I know it. What can we do?"

"Fuck," Andre said.

"I guess we've got a lot of tickets."

"I'll give the ones I've got to Suzanne. She's always up for a good film."

The man had disappeared now, into the life he had worked out, into some back alley that was familiar to him. Perhaps—we hoped—into some protective space. Andre put the car into gear and we circled the empty lot, heading for the exit. Some leaves, left over from fall, blew in a small tornado over that bright, empty tar.

PART FOUR

CHAPTER FORTY-TWO

Andre had assembled twenty-two essays into a collection called *Broken Vessels,* published by David R. Godine of Boston in 1991. *Broken Vessels* had been picked up by a major New York publisher and was now, in June, shortlisted for the Pulitzer Prize. "Dubus writes with searing candor, grace and tenderness," Publishers Weekly reported, ". . .a soul-baring self-portrait, this magical volume contains some of the most personal essays in recent memory."

The title came from an interaction between Andre and his therapist, Judith Tranberg ("Mrs. T"), during the darkest days of Andre's rehabilitation. He'd been working one day with the prosthetic, trying to gain proficiency with a walker, and he had broken down in his efforts. *I'm not a man among men anymore,* he'd said to her, in despair, *and I'm not a man among women, either.*

It's in Jerimiah, Mrs. T told him. *The potter is making a pot and it breaks. So he smashes it and makes a new vessel. You can't make a new vessel out of a broken one. It's time to find the real you.*

•

The MacNeil-Lehrer NewsHour wanted to do an in-studio interview with Andre in Washington, and while there he would have an interview with Terry Gross on a remote link with Philadelphia for her show, *Fresh Air.* Would I go with him? he asked me. I said yes, of course; we'd had many publicity excursions before, but this sounded more important and necessary: we'd always driven to our destinations, even more distant ones, and this would also be my first time flying with Andre.

He certainly needed help with the trip. I looked out the window of my calm Newburyport apartment: there toward the harbor were the Center Congregational Church and the steep rooftops of other apartment buildings and homes. I had just ended a semester at Tufts and had a few days off before my summer semester teaching began in Medford, so the timing was fine. The PR people at the publishing company in New York were taking care of everything, Andre said—we would drive to Logan together and board our flight; at Reagan International Airport a limo would get us and take us to the Duxbury Hotel. The next day we'd be driven to the studio by limo. We'd head to the airport again that afternoon. A quick trip, just there and back.

•

I drove us to Logan International in the Toyota on the day of the flight. We parked on the top floor of long-term parking. I saw someone with an official-looking patch on his shoulder. I lowered the driver's side window.

"My friend here is in a wheelchair and needs handicapped access to the terminal. Can you tell me the best way to go in?"

The man pointed to a set of doors. "That will take you to the terminal you want," he said, in an accent from the Caribbean.

"Thanks."

He nodded. "Have a good day."

We were running just about on time; with no hold-ups, we would make the flight. I got Andre out of the car and we organized our things; Andre took our small suitcases in his lap, securing them with his arms, and I started pushing. We went down the hallway the man had pointed us to, and Andre was joking about something and I was feeling the smooth run of the wheelchair over tile floor and elation that we were finally moving, finally at the airport, we would make it on time, things would be all right. About twenty yards into the hallway there was a turn, and we ran directly into a wall of about ten wide stairs.

"*Shit,*" I said.

"What was that guy talking about?"

There was no way we would make it unless we somehow kept going. I looked over the situation.

"I think I can get you up backwards, buddy," I said.

Andre looked at the stairs. "Fuck it. Let's try it."

I put our suitcases to the side. I reversed the chair and tilted Andre up, then took the chair handles tightly and braced into a wide stance on the second stair. Up one stair, so far so good; up another stair, then one more. I was stepping backward up the staircase, tilting Andre at a steep angle that made him seem, momentarily, weightless on the flat sections. Then I would tighten my back and my legs, and pull the weight of Andre and the wheelchair up each step. As we went up I could see that he was frightened, and suddenly I was, too. With some supreme effort I could pull this off, I thought, but if I was wrong the crash would be horrific, and Andre would have no way to protect himself: he would be a crippled man, half-rolling, half tumbling down those sharp angles. The fear of what I was doing shot through me.

"This isn't smart, buddy," I said, through clenched teeth. I had broken into a heavy, cold sweat. "I won't have the strength to do this."

"That's okay, buddy," Andre said. "Fuck that plane. Let's just go back down easily. No plane is worth this shit."

We got carefully down to safety, the hard, tiled floor seeming like some kind of oasis. I put my hands on my knees and breathed, my head swimming. "That's okay, buddy," Andre said. "Let's take it easy, it's all right now." He always felt like hell when you had to extend yourself to him because of his crippling. It was a kind of shame that washed through him, and he would try to reach out, to help you, somehow. His hand was on my shoulder. "No big fucking deal," he said. My heart pounded in my chest.

We missed the plane, but the airline got us onto another flight. We had been booked first class—Andre's full leg couldn't bend more than sixty-three degrees and had to be braced by pillows, and there was no way to do that in regular passenger seating. But here too, after I got him settled in our 727, we ran into trouble. I tried to put Andre's wheelchair into the small forward-cabin closet where a stewardess had told me to stow it; the wheelchair had to go in there—it couldn't be loose anywhere on the plane. But the closet was jammed with coats, and I struggled to fit it in. The stewardess snapped at me to take it easy, those were a lot of expensive coats and the wheels of the wheelchair would get them dirty. I wasn't about to see Andre, us, treated as an inconvenience: I snapped back that if the airline had accepted Andre's money, they knew his situation and should be able to accommodate him. Finally, exasperated, she gathered some of the coats and put them elsewhere. I didn't give much of a damn, at that point, what happened to those coats.

Andre gripped the handles of his seat tightly as we lifted off, and I thought of his anxiety, especially since the accident, of driving over bridges—the idea of relying on human engineering while suspended *over* something. Flying, I realized now, must be ten times worse. I cursed myself for not thinking of it earlier, not putting up an argument to this excursion. Why the hell hadn't I at least called the airport, the airline beforehand, and checked out handicapped access points and mapped out our route? Why hadn't I been more involved in the planning of this instead of depending on people I didn't know at the distant publishing company? I knew better by now than to trust others who might not have had any true exposure to the lives of the handicapped. Why hadn't the publishing company arranged for a link to a studio in Boston somewhere? What in hell were we doing all of this for?

I told Andre that my father was a pilot and I'd grown up with pilots around me and they were the most competent people I knew. We talked over his anxiety and he visibly calmed down and we went through the nearly two-hour journey that way. The clouds were distant out there beneath the window and the sunlight glowed across the tops of them. The stewardess came by to ask if we were all right, and to chat with us, and we all did our best to smooth things over after the problem with the wheelchair. Andre and I talked for a while and then slept. Then we were descending through clouds, wisps of moisture by the window, feeling the descent in our ears. We seemed to hover over the metropolis. There beyond the plastic oval, rising slowly as the plane banked, were the Jefferson Memorial and the White House.

•

At Reagan International, our limo, promised by the publicity people, never showed up, even though Andre had left them a message about the change in flight. I quickly found a skycap and explained our situation, and he went out to get us a taxi. I looked up at the vast, arched ceiling of the concourse hall, realizing we would have another hurdle here—there was nothing for it but to plunge in and try and make Andre as comfortable as possible. I got us outside to the taxi area and the skycap had waved down a taxi for us and I tipped him. The driver was a Pakistani who stepped out to help and who, when he realized Andre's severe condition, leaned over and said to the skycap, quietly, "I don't want another one like this." Andre didn't hear this: he was already pushing himself toward the car; I helped him into the front passenger seat where he could elevate his leg. I loaded the wheelchair into the trunk, our small suitcases into the back seat beside me, and now as we drove, I guess to combat the taxi driver's insensitivity, I said, "You're sitting next to a man who's on the short-list for the Pulitzer Prize." The taxi driver looked sharply at Andre and I saw the respect I wanted cross his face, but also a new, opportunistic consideration. Soon, the man was telling Andre about the novel he was writing, and how we should maybe all stay in touch.

CHAPTER FORTY-THREE

At the Duxbury Hotel we were tired and hungry, and we put our things into our adjacent rooms and went down the elevator to the main restaurant. The ground floor was smooth as I rolled Andre over it, a pattern of inlaid black diamonds below us. Every inch of the place seemed made of marble or covered with golden leaf. At our table we talked about FDR staying here just before his 1932 inauguration; J. Edgar Hoover, Andre told me, had taken lunch every day for twenty years in another area of the hotel. The round tables were laid out with white linen. We had BLT sandwiches and excellent corn chowder. I looked up at the large chandeliers, at the room around me that held so much Washington history. I imagined all the planning that must have gone into FDR's visit and thought of his resilience: the difficulties he faced with simple movement while also shouldering the presidency in the heart of the Great Depression. I thought of FDR often when I was rolling Andre before me.

•

That evening we left the door open between our rooms and collapsed into sleep. But in the middle of the night I woke and went into Andre's room because his breathing, which I could hear from my bed, was so strange and ragged. He'd had an operation some years before for sleep apnea, and I thought this might have something to do with that; I'd seen him doze before, primarily in the hospital, but never full-on sleep. The light came in the window from the city and Andre lay on his back with pillows supporting various parts of him—the only way he could rest comfortably with the issue of his legs, and he would breathe; the rising and falling of his chest, a slight snore, and then his chest would be still and he would *not* breathe, and it would go on and on. In the shadows of night, it scared me so much I thought something had happened—the exertions of the day had been too much for his heart. Sometimes when he stopped breathing, I feared, momentarily, that he was dying in his sleep. I imagined trying to face his family and everyone he loved after this mess of a trip—telling them he had died on my watch. Then his chest would rise again. I went to the large window. It looked down at Desales Street, down a row of tall, older buildings, a large, lit vertical sign there for ABC News just a few hundred yards ahead. I imagined the activity in that building, even going on at this hour—humanity communicating fiercely through the night; this and the city lights restored some sanity to me. Andre's breathing pattern went on: it was apparently routine for him when he slept deep in the night. Every time his breathing halted, I thought of waking him to make sure he was all right, then realized he probably would not get back to sleep and he needed his rest for the interviews. But I kept my vigil, nodding off occasionally in a chair beside him, into the early hours of morning.

•

We were due at the studio at ten thirty. Andre had arranged with the publishing company for a shower seat to be put in the shower, but when he opened the shower curtain there was a rail on the wall and no shower seat; we looked around the rooms, in the closets, nothing. We both swore at this nightmare beginning all over again. Andre called his publicist, and she got back to us with the news that the hotel didn't have a shower seat immediately available; it wasn't clear where the breakdown in communications had been.

The only way for Andre to shower and for us to be on time was for me to climb in the shower stall with him and hold him from behind, under the armpits, while he tried to wash himself. I got in with my clothes on—I joked with him that I wasn't about to get naked with him, and we'd better make sure there were no cameras around in any case—and then I stepped into the stall and pulled him from his chair onto my thighs, bracing my feet in sneakers hard, carrying Andre's body as best I could—I was a human chair for him, thankful for my strong legs, my years of skiing—and he started the hot spray and washed his hair, his chest, his arms. When he was done his head bent forward with fatigue. I looked through the steam at his sopped gray hair and scalp, his shoulders defeated, the water coming down on us. "This is no good, buddy," he said, above the sound of the spray. "It's no fucking good."

I got him back in his chair, a careful effort. Then while he got ready in his room, I took a shower myself. I'm not sure what I did with my wet clothes—probably threw them out. I wrapped the sneakers in plastic and shoved them in my suitcase: luckily, I had a pair of casual shoes along. I dressed and rushed to get us ready and packed and on time to the interviews. Soon, in a white-walled PBS studio Andre told Terry Gross, an old friend, as they spoke for a few minutes before going on the air, about our trip, that the travel was "horrendous." Then they were into the interview and Terry asked solid, probing questions about his life since the accident, and Andre did his best to answer. But he was exhausted, more than I'd ever heard him be in an interview, his conversational energy a heartbeat behind where it would be normally in such situations. The interview still came off well, because of Terry Gross' preparation and the regard these two had for one another:

TERRY: I think one of the things I'm trying to find out is if you've tried to find a way of telling the story [of the accident] so that people feel ... a larger sense of the fragility of life, do you know what I mean? Like there are ways of telling stories so people feel sorry for you and there are other ways of telling it so that they feel something larger than that.

ANDRE: Every time I tell it to somebody it's always with awe and gratitude. I've met a lot of injured people since my injury, because of the mutual help that we go for. And everyone I know who's crippled has used the words, "gratitude," and "grateful." Because what happened to us was bad enough to have made things worse. So that's always the way I remember it. Well, I remember it with fear, too. And I never lost consciousness and a nurse told me no one remembers the point of impact, but I know two people who do and I'm hoping that I never remember that.

TERRY: Don't you think it's a blessing to not remember—?

ANDRE: Oh, I think it's a great blessing. I remember the headlights and then I remember being on her trunk and then learning that I never lost consciousness, so my eyes must have seen that grill and hood and windshield coming and I'm just very glad I don't remember that.

When Terry asked if literature had helped Andre in his recovery, he answered that he'd read a great deal of the history of the Marines, for the spirit of endurance such books offered him; and he'd relied on great literature, and particularly on the New Testament:

ANDRE: … growing up in Christian Brothers schools as I did—it was a Catholic school—growing up with the passion of Christ as your example of *this is how things are going to be* gives you an expectation of suffering. And then I started reading serious literature when I was about eighteen, and most of that is about, what? People who love each other. People who hurt each other, who lose; so you could say I've been spending most of my spiritual and mental life dealing with suffering of others, from Christ to Natasha in *War and Peace*, right?

I sat quietly beside Andre throughout the remote interview, watching the sound engineer and the producer in the control room, and I admired Andre's ability to rally for this after the trip he'd had. I made a promise to myself that I would question every request on his energy that I knew about from here on in. On the runway, on the plane back to Boston—this time I'd told the stewardesses right away to take out some of the coats and make room for the chair—I sat beside Andre, both of us wiped out. Then we were in the air and Andre said, "I think being crippled in this day and age is a little like being Black in the 1950s—people would prefer you not exist."

CHAPTER FORTY-FOUR

Broken Vessels did not win the Pulitzer Prize, but to Andre, who had never expected the nomination, the overall experience was an inspirational one: he was working steadily now on a new book of essays that would eventually be titled *Meditations from a Movable Chair*. One of these, "Giving Up the Gun," would appear soon in *The New Yorker*.

The essay focuses on a part of Andre's history I'd only imagined: a warm evening in Tuscaloosa in 1985, while I was at Iowa, when Andre was serving a semester as a writing chair at the University of Alabama. As he'd done at Bradford College, Andre often went out with students to bars surrounding the university. On this night, walking with a graduate student just outside a restaurant, Andre witnessed a white man spit out the word "*nigger*" and pull a knife on a black man. It was a charged, dangerous situation: Andre judged it to be a lethal one. He was carrying, in his front jeans pocket, a four-and-a-half-inch-long twenty-two-caliber revolver; he drew the gun, told the white man to back off. But instead of being cowed by the revolver, the man, holding on to his knife, taunted Andre: *Fuck you. Shoot. Go ahead. Shoot.* Cooler heads, the man's friends, intervened; Andre left, profoundly troubled at how close he'd come to shooting and maybe killing a man. The night haunted him.

His history with guns was a long one, he tells his reader in "Giving Up the Gun." He had carried concealed weapons since, years before, "someone I love was raped in Boston by a man who held a knife at her throat." In his formative years in Louisiana "guns in homes were ordinary, where an adult could carry a gun if it was not concealed, and men who worked in woods or swamps often wore holstered handguns so they could shoot snakes." His relationship with guns had changed, however, with the rape. He'd sworn to himself that no woman he was with in a city would ever be violated: "I … did not intend to watch a crucifixion in any form," he writes.

His subsequent night in Alabama challenged the assumptions he'd gone into carrying a concealed weapon with—he'd assumed if he'd ever needed to draw his weapon that the situation would be more simple: he would draw the gun on any man about to assault a woman; he would tell her to call the police while he held his gun on the perpetrator. "This was all very tidy, and I believed it … my confidence … was foolish, and the foolishness was as concealed from my soul as the gun in my pocket or holster was concealed from the eyes of other people."

Five years after that night in Alabama, now in a wheelchair, Andre decided to forgo his dependence on weaponry. "I gave up answers that are made of steel that fire lead, and I decided to sit in a wheelchair on the frighteningly invisible palm of God."

·

The word *surrender* seemed to surface more in his vocabulary now. He spoke of it not as a backing down, but in broad religious terms, as an acceptance of what greater forces had in store for you. "*I have not learned the virtue of surrender—*

which I want—but I have learned the impossibility of avoiding surrender," he writes in "Giving Up the Gun."

The spirit of the word was present in his discussions about guns, and in discussions about the pragmatic trial of his day-to-day living. And in talking about his art. At a library reading we drove to in western Massachusetts one late autumn evening, Andre sat in the chair before his small audience, acting out the drawing back of an arrow in a bow. More and more, he said, he saw in the process of writing a connection to what he'd been reading in books about Zen-Buddhist archery: it was important during creation to lose all sense of the self, of thought, and go where the story and your instincts told you to go—you had to learn to trust where the words were bringing you. The target would draw the arrow to it. Art came from the unconscious mind, and you had to disregard the ego, the propaganda of others telling you how things *should* be, what you *should be interested in,* and trust in your own interests and talent. The commercial aspects of the Western literary world—filling the writer with desires that had nothing to do with art—damaged young, gifted authors before they even had a chance to rise.

•

In another piece for the new book, called "Song of Pity," Andre speaks of a time when he was an undergraduate at McNeese State University, in Louisiana. A sportswriter had come in to give the students a lecture on journalism. Andre thought then that his own future might be as a journalist of some kind, too—that this could support him while he tried his hand, secretly, at fiction writing. The speaker was encouraging, patriotic, inspirational. "Remember," the man said, "the last four letters of American spell *I can.*"

As he neared his sixties now, Andre was on a new journey, the trajectory of his life profoundly altered by the accident that had taken the use of his legs. He'd become impatient with tales of self-reliance that surrounded him, the *I can* promoted by those who wanted to put the best spin on being handicapped; Andre's objection was that this simply wasn't honest—it ignored the basic moment-to-moment living, the survival, the spiritual trial of the individual. "*I sing of those who cannot*," Andre writes, at the end of "Song of Pity":

"To view human suffering as an abstraction, as a statement for how plucky we all are, is to blow air through brass while the boys and girls march in parade off to war. Seeing the flesh as only a challenge to the spirit is as false as seeing the spirit as only a challenge to the flesh. On the planet are people with whole and strong bodies, whose wounded spirits need the constant help that the quadriplegic needs for his body. What we need is not the sound of horns rising to the sky, but the steady beat of the bass drum. When you march to a bass drum, your left foot touches the earth with each beat, and you can feel the drum in your body: *boom* and *boom* and *boom* and *pi*ty *peo*ple *pi*ty *peo*ple *pi*ty *peo*ple."

CHAPTER FORTY-FIVE

It was May, 1993. My aunt Mira and I stepped down from the train that had taken us across Bohemia. The depot sign read *RADNICE:* we were in my father and Mira's childhood village, deep in the heart of Europe, in the Czech Republic. There were the ancient stone walls of the town, the wild grass blowing against the intricate rocks and fences. The pastel townhouses were aged and close: in the slips of space between the buildings you could see gardens cultivated behind. The tall Radnice church rose over the village, the cobblestoned sidewalks were cracked, the tar roads in disrepair after years of neglect under communism. My seventy-one-year-old, good-hearted aunt watched me taking it all in, and told me, "It's a lot for you. You are living in this present life, but you are also living in history, writing scenes in your head."

I was. I called what I was doing "journalism of the heart": my trip had started, I'd hoped, as a project for *National Geographic,* but I'd gradually realized, as I'd gathered my notes in Mira's flat in Prague in the evenings, that what I was working on would be longer than article-length. Since the Velvet Revolution, led by Václav Havel, that had liberated Czechoslovakia from Soviet domination in 1989, Jim McPherson and I had been writing to one another about the possibility of my traveling here. "By all means, Joe, do go," Jim wrote to me in a letter of March 1990. "I saw Havel on television when he was addressing the U.S. Congress. He is an impressive and honest man … I never realized, before now, the kind of gangsters the Soviets are. They have reduced most of the Eastern Europeans to the level of 'niggers.' Now the niggers are talking back. Good. Good. I had deep doubts, before last fall, that the Hand of God was still operating in the affairs of this world. But for the past six months or so, I have been observing miracle after miracle …"

•

Walking these quiet, sunlit streets of Radnice with my aunt now, I remembered all the stories my father had told me on our drives across middle America to deliver our fiberglass shells. Those highway treks—the long rolling days, late-night darknesses, the restless escape of those journeys—had seemed to offer some spiritual protection to my father: his stories had a completeness that I didn't think they would have had in more normal circumstances. The more I'd listened, the more I'd questioned him, Dad seemed to realize he was passing on something important to me, that perhaps I would write about this one day. Now, with the Czech geography all around me, the scenes took form: I could imagine the formative years of my father and aunt here, in this village, in the stability of Tomáš Masaryk's democratic Czechoslovakia. I could see my father and his friends playing soccer on souped-up motorcycles in the fields and learning to ski in the hills in the winters. Then the Munich Conference, the Nazi era, the war. Very little gasoline available and so biking everywhere, wounded Nazis from the Russian front billeted throughout the town, walking these streets; a friendly Wehrmacht colonel who had once been an Olympic track star (his heels had been blown off in battle) on his crutches and watching the boys play soccer, giving them tips from the sidelines.

My father was put to work, aged fifteen, in a coal mine for the Nazi "war effort"—he'd smuggled out sticks of dynamite for use by the Czech Resistance, and hidden them somewhere here on Kalvárie, the small mountain that looked over the church and town. He'd told me about Resistance raids he participated in on trains headed to Terezín—his job, once older members of the Resistance had blown the rails and stopped the train and fought with the Nazi guards, was to pull the Jews out of the cattle car, always at the end of the train, and help bring them to caves for hiding in the forest. These were desperate actions: once the Jewish prisoners had been scattered, the Nazis methodically went about finding them. My father had a haunting memory of opening train doors and discovering that some of the people in those terribly packed cars had suffocated and died in transit standing up.

•

Dad told me—on a long night with highway lines rushing before us, stark gas stations with giant American flags lit and waving—about the five different communist prisons he was held in when he'd refused to cooperate with the Stalinists, and they'd suspected him of spying for the Americans. How, on the door of his prison cell at Pankrác prison in Prague, a prisoner of the earlier, Nazi regime had written, *Believe that your suffering is not in vain—1942.* And a prisoner of the subsequent communist regime had written, *But it sure as hell was in vain—1949.*

After my father's release he'd joined a *skupina*, or Underground group, and taken on missions to guide Czech democratic statesmen to freedom in night-long, difficult hikes over the Sumava Mountains, to Germany, slipping by the communist patrols. He'd helped save the Czech democratic presidential contender and economist, Dr. Josef Macek, and his wife, Běla, this way. Then Dad had been shot in an ambush in Prague, escaped with a bullet in his collarbone, and the Underground had arranged for an operation and finally smuggled him through safehouses until he walked over the mountains to freedom himself, one last time.

•

I walked in Dad's footsteps. In Bohemia, I always had a notebook with me. I wrote in Radnice, Mira and I staying with family friends, and in nearby Žebrak, the town where many of my cousins resided. I wrote extensively in Mira's flat on Vinohradská in Prague. I wrote on trams and buses. I would stop to write notes at a bench while my aunt rested and clarified things for me and made sure I understood her translations. It was Mira who suggested I interview Father Václav Malý, the famous dissident priest and a leader of the "Velvet Revolution." She told me she had been in the audience with three quarters of a million people in November 1989, at Prague's Letná stadium, when Father Maly, presiding over the demonstration, brought forth two agents of the secret police; they apologized for the terror they had inflicted on their country.

"It was such a moment," Mira said. "There was anger in the many people there, and I wondered—would things become violent? When the men had finished, Father Maly went to the microphone and said, Our Father—'"

Three quarters of a million people said, "*Who art in heaven ...*"

•

"I wanted to attract attention to the fact that without God's blessing, our actions wouldn't be possible," Václav Malý told me, on the morning we met outside his St. Anton church in Prague. The priest was in a striped sports shirt and casual slacks, and the tram went by us so loudly sometimes we had to pause. "That the revolution was not only done through Havel and his friends but that it was above all a matter of heaven. It was a very special feeling, a very strange feeling, because of the risk involved that I would be rejected. That it was successful wasn't my merit but the merit of God."

Václav Malý had for many years lived in defiance of the communist state. He was arrested and interrogated some two hundred and fifty times. He was beaten, imprisoned, harassed, forced to labor in the new underground subway system the Soviets were installing in Prague.

When I asked him for a definition of courage, Maly laughed a little, modestly, then seemed to look for the best answer he could give me. "Above all to live a one-faced life," he said. "To have something inside and reflect this *outside*. And not only to reflect the truth in the heart but to live according to the truth."

•

On a gray, overcast day, Mira and I walked up and down outside the eastern concrete wall of Pankrác prison. I was thinking of my father here, and of the many who had been brutalized, and who had died here. In Nazi times, political prisoners in Pankrác were executed by beheading or hanging, or by being sent to firing squads or concentration camps. During communist times they were hung or brought to labor in a nearby uranium mine, a slow death sentence. I thought of the prisoners who had been beaten, starved, thrown into freezing rooms for days on end, all for some abstract political philosophy, for maniacal leaders with power-hungry ambitions. I grieved for all these political prisoners. Dad had been accused of treason here, had endured beatings in interrogations, waited for death to come. Even though someone in the Party had finally believed his story of innocence, a kangaroo court was set up to accuse him of a series of lesser crimes to justify his incarceration: the Party could not be wrong.

My aunt told me that we were on the same place that my grandmother had walked, pacing, praying for her son. Sometimes my grandmother heard the carpentry, the scaffolding being built for hangings. A clock tower, painted red, rose over the wall we walked beneath. In communist times, on the nights before executions, the bells of the clock were silenced, letting the condemned know that they had little time left in the world.

CHAPTER FORTY-SIX

In Newburyport, over seven years, I wrote nineteen drafts of a book tentatively called *Fields of Light*. I got my title from a Bohemian legend Mira had told me about: that the warriors of the fourteenth-century Prince Wenceslas would rise from the fields to defend the nation in danger. I sensed in the legend my father's story, and the story of all those who suffered under totalitarianism—their collective spirit was still in the blood of their home.

I was using as my models *Balkan Ghosts,* by Robert Kaplan, and a book that Young Andre suggested, the powerful *Goodbye Darkness,* by William Manchester. Both of these works found the authors braiding intense personal and political history. My book was a travelogue—a portrait of the Czech Republic in 1993—but it was primarily a story of my father and family. The communists had eliminated my father from the history of his native land: I'd decided that *Fields of Light* would be my effort to write him back into that history.

Andre was reading my work, discussing the project with me, especially as I neared completion. We got into heavy conversations en route to Showcase Cinemas.

"I think you need more of the chapter of the Father Maly interview," he told me once, as I was nearing my final draft.

"That's not because I'm a Catholic and I want to see more of him, though I do," he said. He paused as I threaded the Toyota onto the exit from 110 onto 495 South. "But because first, the book needs more reflective pacing there, and more importantly you can feel Father Maly setting an overall spiritual tone for the work at that point, toward the end."

"I was afraid I might be overwhelming the reader with the interview, throwing the whole thing into imbalance—"

"I don't think you'll be overwhelming the reader at all. Even just in terms of the music of the book, you need more of that section—"

"Father Maly spoke of doing hard labor, that it put him in touch with the working man—he said how valuable that was. He said the communist times taught him that when one accepts one's limitations, one is truly free. I thought maybe I'd add that."

Andre looked at me, the highway running through part of his glasses. "That's important, buddy. That belongs in there."

Fields of Light, when finished, went through two agents (both connections arranged by Andre) and was considered by a number of publishers and consistently rejected. Though it sometimes came close to being taken, I inevitably heard a familiar response: the editors didn't know how to categorize it and consequently they felt it wouldn't sell, much as they liked the writing. The rejections piled up, and sometimes I just gave in to the thought that it would never be published. I admitted to Andre one night that I was fighting despair as a result. Andre sympathized, but encouraged me to keep trying and not let my artistic output be affected by the depression. *The real victory*, he said, *is the manuscript finished and on the desk, as true as you can make it. The rest will take care of itself.*

I went for long one-in-the-morning walks through the seaport to distract myself from my constant lack of success. I went through Market Square, empty on the late summer nights, brick walkways and a minimum of lights in the shops of State Street, all waiting for the morning and the tourists that would come. I told myself that I had at least produced something for my family, a history they could turn to when they spoke of my father in the years and generations ahead. By telling the story I had honored Dad, I hoped: Dad had seemed moved, in his reserved way, (he and Mom were in semi-retirement now) by the manuscript when I'd last visited him and the family. There was that to think about, no small thing. I looked at the windows of the bookstores, at the newest publications standing proudly behind the glass.

•

After the second agent had sent me his regrets—it wasn't really worth his time to keep trying, he said, he was very sorry (I even sensed he was mad with Andre for having pushed my project onto him) two dozen roses showed up at the door of my Newburyport apartment. Andre's note said, *Keep fishing, Santiago.*

I sent the manuscript to publishers on my own. The rejection count reached nearly forty. It was Young Andre's idea to have his father nominate *Fields of Light* for the Pushcart Editors' Book Award, a recognition for the best unpublished book of the year. Andre did so, and I thanked father and son for their faith and was soon absorbed again by my teaching and correcting papers and preparing send-outs of *Fields of Light,* and the rejections that came, steadily, to my mailbox. *Fields of Light* was held over by Pushcart in 1999, and it won the contest the following year; it would be published by Pushcart/W.W. Norton. But by the time I heard this news, my mentor would be gone.

CHAPTER FORTY-SEVEN

I have this memory that comes back to me when I think of Andre in his last years. The two of us driving to Boston for a reading of his at Boston Public Library. We were surprised to see, on the late summer day, that the line to get in the reading went around the block. People waited patiently, copies of Andre's latest books in their hands or held against their chests for autographing later.

Backstage in the auditorium, we heard the hushed, busy tones of the packed audience and Andre told me that were a lot of people out there, that he felt more nervous than usual. "No need to be, buddy," I said. "You always do well at these things. Except for that time in Amherst—you remember? When your nerves got the best of you and you just *fucked things up*—"

He threw back his head and laughed. "Your timing is excellent, as usual, you *bastid*," he said. He was still smiling and shaking his head as I rolled him out on stage. The audience—over three hundred people—rose to give him a standing ovation; this too surprised us, and I had to fight back tears.

I got back behind the curtains and watched and made sure Andre was all right, then took the stairs down the back way to the lecture hall. The only spot I could find where I didn't intrude on somebody's vision was toward the back, standing. From there, Andre was a small figure in his wheelchair, his glasses down on his nose, reading to the silent audience, and I had the strange, soaring sense of something big happening, a certainty that my friend was going into history.

•

Evenings in Newburyport in December 1998, were filled with Christmas lights, strung over the streets and in the sidewalk trees, and surrounding the brick doorways of the many shops. The shops were lit brightly: eclectic clothing stores and shoe and eyeglass and furniture places, a stainless-steel kitchen shop and antique stores and a sea-salt, bath-and-spa-products establishment. There were the smells of soaps and candles and pine. Fowles Soda and Cigars Diner, circa 1903, still looked as if it were living in that distant age except for the multitude of new, glossy magazines that lined its walls. Outside, on the brick walkways, there was the strong, fresh smell of the ocean. The city was crowded all day with shoppers, often snow coming down, but evenings in the seaport at this time of year were magical. Beyond the waterfront boardwalk there was the gunmetal gray of the bay, the wind creating whitecaps, in the distance the spit of Plum Island where the Merrimack River met the sea.

I was seeing a young woman named Allison Lee—she had once been my student at Emerson College. Allie came from New York state and had moved to Newburyport recently: she already had a job teaching Freshman English at Northern Essex Community College. She was beautiful, with wheat-blond hair and gray-blue eyes, an excellent writer. She had a dry wit that could catch you off guard and make you laugh, suddenly, at her observations. In her early twenties, Allie handled finances far better than I could—(she was frequently disappointed by my financial habits)—it was breathtaking to me, the way she bought things on her VISA card, then switched the balance back and forth to another credit card monthly to avoid paying interest. She was paying off a brand-new Honda Civic this way. One night at Andre's home Allie ordered pizza for the three of us, and Andre said he was pretty sure she had it worked out that Honda was paying for the pizza.

He adored her. When I couldn't get away from my work to go to films, they went together, and Allie accompanied Andre to readings, and once to WBUR in Boston for a radio broadcast—they called me happily from the limo on their way home to recap the high points of the interview. Privately, Andre tried to convince me, on a few occasions, to marry Allie. Other friends did the same, commenting on her beauty, saying they don't come by like that too often. Part of me was afraid to take that leap—but I see now that I was also becoming more and more absorbed in a war against anxiety that I'd carried with me all my life and that now was manifesting itself not only in my superstitions and compulsive behavior but in a kind of moral policing of the world—a problem that would take me many years to contend with. In movie theatres, I would get up and tell people to please stop their g-damned talking, especially when I saw that it was bothering Allie and Andre. It amazed me that people wouldn't just be civil when the lights went down and *shut up*. In supermarkets I would collect products that were past expiration and go make an issue of it with the manager: I could imagine children eating tainted food, getting sick while the supermarket made its profit. If I saw a child mistreated in public, I would intervene, then shadow the family and get a license plate and call children's services in Massachusetts with a report. If I saw someone parked in a handicapped spot who didn't belong there, I would hound them until they drove off, swearing at me. I didn't like all the conflict—feared it, in fact—but the idea that an innocent person would suffer for someone else's convenience, someone else's unjust behavior, made me crazy.

Sometimes in the aftermath of these incidents I couldn't catch a breath, no matter how hard I tried. It was like there was a small corner of one lung that just didn't open enough to take in air. Teaching, much as I enjoyed the students, seemed to be causing a lot of the anxiety, too. I would get wrapped up in the dramatic and sometimes traumatic stories of their lives. One night, coming home late from Emerson, I had a breathing attack and, on the highway, felt the world narrowing in focus. I leaned back in the seat, tried to relax. Got to an exit, an abandoned parking lot, parked a while and closed my eyes until I felt normal again and was breathing steadily and my head stopped spinning. I made it home safely but realized that this problem was growing, that I would have to fix it, somehow.

Something Jim McPherson had written to me once came back to me, frequently, now: *My own feeling,* he'd said, *is that your father passed values onto you that you now have a responsibility to dramatize.*

"About a week ago," I told Andre—we were at a restaurant called Glenn's Galley on the waterfront of Newburyport, Andre, Jack Herlihy, Allie, and me—"I was at the post office, and just after I'd parked this guy pulled into a handicapped spot on Pleasant street and ran up the stairs. I followed him in and went up to him where he was, at the end of this long line, and told him that a lot of people needed that spot and he said '*Cool it*,' and that put me into this sudden *rage*. I said I wouldn't cool it, I would get the police, and he left the line and walked fast to his car, and I walked beside him, telling him what I thought of him. He slammed the door and sped off. I was shaking for the rest of the day."

"Sometimes his breathing really gets bad—" Allie said, sliding her hand onto my forearm. "It seems to be worse in the hours *after* these things happen."

"You make yourself too available to people, buddy, to the *world*," Andre said to me, thoughtfully. "You remember what I was like at the end of teaching? There's a lot of pressure on you. You need to cut yourself off from things a little more, get an unlisted number so you don't feel "on call" all the time. Do yoga, or tai-chi, or some relaxation discipline. The problem isn't so much *what* you're doing—you're just being a moral man—as the way you're doing it and how you're letting it affect you." Allie nodded her head with this: she had been telling me the same things, and she was glad my mentor was telling me them, too.

Andre suggested therapy, which I was, inexplicably, too proud to do. I took his advice about getting a new, unlisted number, though, and started doing beginner's yoga to tapes with Patricia Walden, and exercising more. And Andre helped me organize a new schedule, sitting at his dining table with me one day, writing my commitments on the back of an envelope. My teaching and correcting load was so heavy, he said—a graduate class this semester at Emerson, two upperclassman writing classes now per semester at Tufts, a lot of driving back and forth to Boston, a lot of reading and commenting on student work, week after week—that I was having trouble getting to my own writing. He knew I had to write, even if my time for my art was limited. "Even if you schedule just three times a week for your own work at forty minutes each," Andre told me, going over it all with me, "you'll be more calm because you'll know you're getting it done."

Andre gave me self-help books that he'd used himself in the past to deal with his own hypertension and anxiety: of these I remember in particular *The Relaxation Response,* written by Dr. Herbert Benson, of the Harvard Medical School. Benson gave an education on the physical effect of stress on the body, and was insistent that controlled meditation, done twice a day, would lower blood pressure and anxiety. I combined the practice, eventually, with the end of my yoga sessions.

I worked on my fiction four early mornings a week; I composed songs on the F-50. Allie and I walked, bundled up, on the windy shore of Plum Island. This all helped. Still, I had the breathing attacks in times of pressure and anxiety; still, caught up in my own drama, I took my relationship with the beautiful Allie for granted.

CHAPTER FORTY-EIGHT

There was a lot of snow that year when winter came. Bill Cantwell—Young Andre's lifelong friend from Haverhill and a close confidant of the Dubus family—and I fell into a habit of showing up as the storms were finishing to shovel Andre's zigzagging handicapped ramp. Bill was built wide and strong, a seven-time judo blackbelt; he was also a Pulitzer Prize winning editor for *The Lawrence Eagle Tribune.* He came to every task, it seemed, with a positive spirit. Since the accident he'd been enormously helpful to Andre. Once, when Andre and I got stuck in the Toyota on the ice in Andre's driveway, I'd called Bill, then watched him drive up, get out of his car with a nod and a cheerful wave, and step over and crouch and lift the Toyota at the front, swiveling the 2500-lb machine onto dry tar.

Over the years Bill had become my close friend—he called me Jose-Can-You-See—and I always thought of him as a rock, grateful for his presence, especially in difficult times. We usually started at different points of the handicapped ramp, working toward each other, knifing our shovels down into the thick cover and lifting and tossing over the rails. Bill shoveled snow like a locomotive—two shovelfuls to my every one. He treated the job as a pleasant workout, and I watched sometimes amazed at how fast the white stuff kept flying over the railing. Our breaths rose into the air. Occasionally we shouted out comments about the heaviness or lightness of the snow and the newest gossip about our friends or the Red Sox or the Patriots. Andre would open up the door—"Hey, hey, Billy C! Hey, hey, Buddy!"—and tell us how grateful he was and engage us in some conversation to give us a break, offering us glasses of water. If it was warmer Andre often left the door open and worked in his kitchen while we shoveled, his way of being with us, providing companionship, as we labored. We cleared away the ramp and the railings and the area around Andre's car, then started on the two decks.

•

Late February now, 1999: I returned from grocery shopping to a message from Andre—would I want to come by and see a film tonight?—he'd just hooked up some new speakers to the television, *So it'll sound like we're in Showcase Cinemas,* he told me. *But I know you probably can't make it,* he said. *I know you have to teach tomorrow.* When I called him back, I got his message machine and confirmed that I would need to drive to Tufts in the morning. *I'm anxious to hear those new speakers soon, though,* I said.

Andre was one of the only people at that point who had my new number: I was slowly getting around to giving it to my closest friends. That night I woke from sleep to the otherworldly ringing of my phone. It was just past eleven. I got out of bed and heard my message machine in the front hallway answer and then a woman's voice, an operator, saying, *Mr. Hurka, there is a Bill Cantwell who urgently needs to reach you, could you call him back at this number—?* She hung up just as

I reached the phone. It immediately rang again. I picked up: Bill Cantwell's somber voice was on the line.

"Bill, what's this, what's happened?"

"It's bad news, brother. Are you sitting down?"

"No, but go ahead and tell me, I'm all right. What's happened?"

"It's Andre the Elder—" this was how Bill distinguished the Andres one from the other "—Andre died tonight."

Bill told me: Andre had also invited his son, Jeb, and Bob Talman, another mutual friend who worked at carpentry with Jeb, over to see the film. Bob had arrived first and gone into the house, where he heard the shower running steadily. The water seemed to go on for an unusually long time with no other sound or movement. Bob knocked and called out, then went into the bathroom and found Andre sitting on his amputee's bench, leaning with his head against the wall. The shower water was cool. He'd had a massive heart attack; the EMTs arrived in moments, but Andre was gone.

·

After I hung up with Bill I called Allie. I told her how Andre had died, and then the details of the night blur: I have a memory of holding Allie on the sidewalk outside her apartment, stars scattered above, talking about my friend. It seems to me then that we returned to my apartment soon after, the lights in the living room blazing through the night, seeming to be all on at the wrong time. We spoke in hushed tones, in deference to those in the apartments below and above. Much later, toward dawn, I found myself on my knees, Allie holding her arms tightly around me from behind, saying things to try and calm me down.

CHAPTER FORTY-NINE

Two mornings after Andre's death, very early, I was on the North Shore train moving through the pale whiteness of the New England winter. I had been asked by a WBUR radio show, *The Connection,* to join the host, Christopher Lydon, in a memorial-and-celebration broadcast of Andre's life and work. I frankly didn't want to interrupt my grief with this, but the producer, Louie Cronin, was a dear friend of mine and, just recently, Andre had told me that Christopher Lydon, who he'd done shows with before, was a good man, a serious literary man. I watched the New England towns go by, thinking of all those years ago when I was traveling on this train to see Andre after his accident. I remembered Andre's courage; I watched the sunlight breaking low through the buildings, across the snowy expanses of parking lots. I looked down at two of Andre's books that I'd brought with me to quote on the show if needed: *Meditations from a Movable Chair* and *Dancing After Hours,* his last short story collection; I opened *Meditations* and turned the pages, stopping and rereading passages that I'd marked.

In humid air, Andre wrote, in an essay called "Sacraments," *the leaves would be darker, but now they are bright, and you can see lighted space between them, so that each leaf is distinct; and each leaf is receiving sacraments of light and air and water and earth. So am I, in the breeze on my skin, the air I breathe, the sky and earth and trees I look at.*

His words had a new weight to them, as if they were set in stone now.

•

In the studio at Boston University, I sat at a table with Christopher Lydon, while Louie, in the control booth, fielded an avalanche of calls. We spent the fast hour collecting remembrances from writers, friends and fans. I read a quote that Gina Berriault had given me, the day before, to say on the air (she'd been too emotional to go on herself)—*Andre was the most heartfelt writer I've ever known.* Listeners asked questions and offered observations: Jessica Treadway, from our Thursday night workshop group, called in to offer a personal advertisement that Andre had written, a decade before, when he was gathering the courage to date again:

SWM, 52, good physical condition except for amputated left leg and crippled right one, largely confined to wheelchair, fiction writer, divorced father of six who despises money and is presently living on credit, seeks companionship of female with or without children, who loves the sea, beaches, woods, sky, weather, drinking in bars, jazz and country and opera, lying idly in the sun, reading fiction and poetry, a spurner of psychobabble and psychotherapy, who strives for a spiritual life while remaining hedonistic; must be witty and kind, good to my six-year-old and eighteen-month-old daughters, resilient and passionate; must not love money and things but must enjoy smoking and other such pleasures of the flesh, like daylight and nocturnal lovemaking, and pleasurable distractions like movies and idle talk, and must have a car 'til I can buy one. Honesty absolutely required, and spontaneous justified and even loud and obscene anger are not essential but would season the relationship. This is not all fun in the sun but a durable graceful dance to the music of mortality. Former nuns of light heart are welcome.

CHAPTER FIFTY

That evening there was a large gathering at Young Andre and his wife Fontaine's apartment in Newburyport. Young Andre, having just started his book tour for his new novel, *House of Sand and Fog,* had flown home from San Francisco. Family and friends came in from all over. It was crowded and there was a lot of emotion. I saw Bill Cantwell across the room with his wife Rene, and Allie and I went over to them.

"Bill, thanks for being the one to tell me," I said.

Bill's eyes widened. "To tell you, brother—?"

"Your phone call to tell me about Andre—"

"Joe," Bill said, "I didn't *talk* to you." Rene's eyes were wide now, too. Others gathered around us, feeling something in the air. Bill said, "We asked the operator to get a message to you, because she said your old number was no longer valid."

"I got her call," I said. "But then the phone rang, and you were there, telling me what happened."

"Joe, I swear, I didn't talk to you."

"Wait a minute," Philip Spitzer, Andre's agent, said. "There's some explanation. One of you may have been in shock and may not be remembering—"

"I swear," Bill said to all of us, again. "We didn't talk to Joe that night. We all made a list of a few people to call—" Rene was affirming this "—and Joe was on our list and the operator said the new number was unlisted and she could only leave a message for us."

"And I'm just as sure we spoke," I said. Allie was nodding. "I told Allie everything right after. I told my family early the next morning. How would I have known all that if you hadn't communicated it to me?"

To this day, we have no explanation for this mystery.

•

Soon, within a day or two, it snowed again. Without coordinating it, Bill and I showed up within minutes of one another at Andre's home. We shoveled for a long while, clearing the handicapped ramp, the area where the Toyota sat. Finally, Bill had to go. He gave me a bear hug, asked if I was all right, and I said sure, no worries, I'll just hang around a little longer, thank you, Bill—and I watched as he backed down the driveway.

I could feel Andre all around me: the suddenness of his leaving the earth was still astonishing. Fragments of things he'd told me came back to me. Once, when I was an undergraduate, I'd asked him what he truly felt about the afterlife. *Oh, I think there's something there,* he'd told me, with certainty: *there's too much rage and passion in a human being to bury into the earth.*

I paced by his car, cleaning off his mirrors with a broom, wiping down the windows as if Andre were just inside the house, and we were getting ready to go to Showcase Cinemas. I absently pushed the shovel and cleared away snow that was whitening the surrounding ground, and I thought with some bitterness about the prizes my friend should have won, imagined him moving forward, dressed better than I'd ever seen him be, accepting a medal in Stockholm. *You deserved all of that and more, Andre,* I told him. He had died way too early, aged only sixty-two; this was all devastating, unfair. But then his voice was telling me that what I was wishing for—the prizes and accolades—were of least importance: that *the real victory is the manuscript finished and on the desk, as true as you can make it—*

The snow was intensifying. Everything except Andre's car was white or black or gray. The Toyota looked tired, a corner of the wheelchair box rusting. The whiteness quickly covered the car, the tar surrounding it, the railings and ramp Bill and I had just shoveled. Birds called briefly, lighting a moment on the telephone lines, then swooping into the snowfall. After the birds it was quiet, with only the steady sound of the precipitation. I put the shovel and broom back in the Honda and hesitated before driving home. I kept standing there.

I couldn't bring myself to leave him, not just yet.

SELECTED BIBLIOGRAPHY

Benson, Herbert, M.D. *The Relaxation Response*. New York: Avon Books, 1976.

Blumenthal, Michael. *Against Romance*. New York: Viking/Penguin, 1987.

Chekhov, Anton. *How To Write Like Chekhov*. DaCapo Press, 2008.

Chekhov, Anton. *Anton Chekhov*. 18 volumes. New York: The Echo Press, 1985.

Dodd, Susan. *Old Wives' Tales*. Iowa City, Iowa: University pf Iowa Press, 1984.

Dubus, Andre. *Separate Flights*. New Hampshire: David R, Godine, Publisher, 1975.

Dubus, Andre. *Selected Stories*. New York: Vintage Books, 1996.

Dubus, Andre. *Meditations From A Movable Chair*. New York: Vintage, 1998.

Dubus, Andre. *Broken Vessels*. Boston: David R. Godine, Publisher, 1991.

Dubus, Andre. *The Last Worthless Evening*. Boston: David R, Godine, Publisher, 1986.

Dubus, Andre. *The Times Are Never So Bad*. Boston: David R, Godine, Publisher, 1983.

Hurka, Joseph. *Fields Of Light: A Son Remembers His Heroic Father*. New Hampshire: Wild Creek Press, 2013. Pushcart Editors' Book Award, 2001.

McPherson, James Alan. *Elbow Room*. New York: Fawcett-Crest, 1975. Winner of the Pulitzer Prize.

McPherson, James Alan. *A Region Not Home: Reflections From Exile*. New York: Simon & Schuster, 2000.

Pancake, Breece DJ. *The Stories Of Breece DJ Pancake*. Holy McDougal, 1984.

Wiesel, Elie. *The Night Trilogy*. New York: Hill and Wang, 1985.

Yates, Richard. *The Collected Stories Of Richard Yates*. New York: Picador/Henry Holt and Company, 2001.

ACKNOWLEDGEMENTS

With my great thanks to those who supported this effort and helped me remember: Lori Ambacher, Mary Bevilacqua, Joshua Bodwell, Paul Bourque, Bill Cantwell, Sam Cornish, Louie Cronin, Susan Dodd, Suzanne Dubus, Andre Dubus III, Joan Esposito, Patrice Gerrior, Sylva Boyadjian-Haddad, Farid Haddad, Heather Heckman-McKenna, DeWitt Henry, Jack Herlihy, Aditi Kocherlakota, Rachel McPherson, Maura MacNeil, Maggie Martin, Jennifer Militello, Dr. Shaheen Mozaffar, Dr. Patricia O'Malley, Terry O'Malley, Michele Perkins, George Rosen, Patrick Samway, Carolyn Seymour, Rachael Stewart, Enid Thuermer, Carol Thomas, Jim Thompson, Jessica Treadway, Kathy Tully, Sandra Tyler, Petr Valta, and Carol Wilkinson.

My gratitude, as well, goes out to my newfound kindred spirits at Vine Leaves Press: Jessica Bell, Ashley Crantas, Amie McCracken, and Alexis Paige. All were gracious and inspirational as we developed this book together.

Finally, a big thank you to my family—for their steady encouragement, faith, strength, and love.

VINE LEAVES PRESS

Enjoyed this book?
Go to *vineleavespress.com* to find more.
Subscribe to our newsletter:

www.ingramcontent.com/pod-product-compliance
Ingram Content Group UK Ltd.
Pitfield, Milton Keynes, MK11 3LW, UK
UKHW012253290726
14090UKWH00016B/621

9 783988 321534